MORE BIG WORDS FOR OUR TIME

A LIFT FOR THE LIVING

and

A GIFT FOR THE GRIEVING

By
W. Hamp Watson, Jr.
With Dr. J. Frederick Wilson

CWP

CAMBRIDGE WAY PUBLISHING

❖ **TO PLACE AN ORDER**
OR TO INQUIRE ABOUT BECOMING A SALES OUTLET,
AND FOR RIGHTS AND PERMISSIONS REQUESTS,
CONTACT:

W. Hamp Watson, Jr. Editor
CAMBRIDGE WAY PUBLISHING
149 Cambridge Way
Macon, Georgia 31220-8736
SAN: 255-8041
Email whwatson2@cox.net
Tel: (478) 475-1763

◆ ◆ ◆

❖ **THE SALES PRICE: $14.00**
Proceeds from all sales will benefit Wesley Glen Ministries,
Incorporated, 4850 N. Mumford Road, Macon, Georgia 31210. If
purchased at a United Methodist Church of the South Georgia
Conference or an institution of the Conference, there will be no
additional charge. Add $2.00 for shipping and handling if ordered
from Cambridge Way Publishing.

Cover design by Lillian Davis

Scripture quotations noted RSV are from the Revised Standard Version of
the Bible, copyrighted 1946, 1952, 1971, 1973 by the Division of Christian
Education of the National Council of the Churches of Christ in the U.S.A.,
and are used by permission. Quotations noted KJV are from the King
James Version of the Bible.

ISBN 0-9746976-1-3

To our children:
Susan Watson Bagwell,
Wade Hampton Watson, III,
and Ann Watson
who have been there for
their mother and me
during our recent crises

❖

ACKNOWLEDGEMENTS

Thanks to:

- ❖ Contributors who gave the funds for the cost of printing so that proceeds from all sales of the book could be given to Wesley Glen Ministries, Incorporated, a network of group homes sponsored by The South Georgia Conference of The United Methodist Church to serve "Adults with Disabilities."
- ❖ Mr. and Mrs. John R. Batts for providing the tape for "Tribulation."
- ❖ Mrs. Eunice Brown for providing the tape of Dr. Frederick Wilson's Funeral Meditation for her son, Dr. L. E. Brown.
- ❖ Dr. Fred Craddock for stories and material cited on the pages they are used and for his insights on the cover regarding Dr. Frederick Wilson's preaching.
- ❖ Lillian Davis of Macon, Georgia for designing the Front and Back Covers and giving other invaluable assistance.
- ❖ Katherine Johnson and Victoria Logue, daughters of Dr. Frederick Wilson, for editing some of his messages.
- ❖ Brendan Martin, grandson of Mrs. Eunice Brown, for providing a CD for Dr. Wilson's messages on Balance, Compassion, Example, and Sacrifice.
- ❖ Carol Maynard for making copies of the manuscript to mail to the printer.
- ❖ Dr. William "Billy" Oliver, President/CEO of Wesley Glen for his support and encouragement.
- ❖ Dr. A. Jason Shirah for his endorsement on the cover.
- ❖ Dr. J. Frederick Wilson for much of the content of "Forgiveness." With the tape destroyed, I wrote this from my memory of his approach to the message. So much of it is his that I included it in the front section with his messages.

W. Hamp Watson, Jr.

Contents

INTRODUCTION

Why *More Big Words for Our Time?* This book is in some sense a sequel. My first book was *Frederick Wilson Still Speaks – Big Words for Our Time.* In that book, I edited eight sermons of tapes that I had heard the late Dr. Frederick Wilson preach. I also included one message of mine based on notes I had made after hearing him. Sales benefited the Methodist Home for Children and Youth, an institution Dr. Wilson loved.

More Big Words for Our Time includes six more messages from Frederick that surfaced as people graciously shared with me other tapes of his that they had kept and treasured across these years since he died in 1990. In examining these messages I determined that they were focused primarily on giving hope to people that were going through trying times or loss of loved ones. I decided to add ten *Big Word* messages of my own to create a little volume that would be suitable for two purposes: (1) A Lift for the Living, and (2) A Gift for the Grieving.

I was led to this emphasis by a conversation I had with Carol Maynard, longtime Secretary at Martha Bowman Memorial United Methodist Church, Macon, Georgia. She was graciously assisting me by making copies of another book that I was mailing to a potential publisher. She said, "When my father died my mother really had a difficult time. I looked everywhere to find some book that would be helpful to her in her grief, but the only thing I could find at that time was Catherine Marshall's book, *"I'll See You In the Morning"*. I wish you would write a book that really spoke to that need."

The book begins with "Remembering Frederick Wilson", a Memorial Service I conducted at Vineville United Methodist Church in Macon, Georgia fourteen years after the death of this beloved pastor. Some of the messages that follow examine the whole grieving and renewal experience for people. One message is actually a funeral sermon delivered by Dr. Wilson. The book concludes with the big word, "Perseverance—In Times Like These", a reflection on 9/11 that I delivered to my little congregation at Glenwood Hills near the time of that tragedy.

A conversation with the Reverend C. E. "Ned" Steele whose daughter, Sandra, is one of God's "Special Persons" led me to want all sales of this new book to benefit Wesley Glen. Wesley Glen Ministries, Incorporated is the network of group homes sponsored by the South Georgia Conference of the United Methodist Church for "Adults with Disabilities". Ned said, "You've done that book to benefit the Children's Home, why don't you do something for Wesley Glen?"
Dr. William "Billy" Oliver, President/CEO of Wesley Glen, has given his approval to this project.

IT is my hope that there will be persons now on the shining side of life who will use this book to prepare themselves to walk with confident faith through the crises that they are now experiencing and through the shadows that are coming someday for us all. I even harbor the hope that as grieving people read they will be helped to move from mourning to morning, from darkness to light.

W. Hamp Watson, Jr.

REMEMBRANCE
"Remembering Frederick Wilson"
Memorial Sermon by Hamp Watson at Vineville United
Methodist Church, Macon, Georgia, fourteen years after
Dr. Frederick Wilson's death
I Corinthians 1:12-13, 3:4-7, Philippians 1:3
"I thank my God in all my remembrance of you."

Paul began his letter to the church at Philippi by saying, *"I thank my God in all my remembrance of you."* But that phrase is more than the beginning of a letter. Chuck Thompson, who did the story on the book in the Macon Telegraph, asked me how it was that I came to write my first book, Frederick Wilson Still Speaks – Big Words for Our Time, and I tried to come up with a few reasons. I told him, "Well, I tried for twenty years to get Frederick to publish and he was so self effacing that he wouldn't do it. He truly did not think his sermons were worthy of publication. But I knew they were. I was retired and serving such a small church that I had enough time to do it. As technologically challenged as I've always been, my brother-in-law forced me to learn to use a computer by giving me one; and suddenly I had some of the skills to do it. Then I thought that the sales could benefit the children's home that he loved. And I had the permission from his daughters that I had never been able to get from him while he was alive."

But you know how you look back on an interview and realize what you should have said? I should have borrowed Paul's words. The real reason I wrote this book, the real motivation for doing it was this, "I thank my God in all my remembrance of Frederick Wilson," and this was a way to get that expressed. This was a way to say it to as many people as I could. It had been burning in my bones since the day he died.

I knew I was not by myself in having this feeling and I really discovered it when I started getting orders in the mail for the books. People don't just order the books. Oh some do who don't know they're writing the author when they write Cambridge Way Publishing, but the majority of the orders come with a single page or sometimes a two page letter telling what Frederick Wilson meant to them. Bishop Marion Edwards' brother Joe, retired from the North Georgia Conference, writes telling how Frederick led him into the ministry just by the Sermons he preached when Joe was attending Georgia Teachers College at Statesboro. That's Georgia Southern now. A woman calls to order one and nearly tells me over the phone the entire funeral sermon he preached for her Doctor son.

So when Nancy Todd asked me to speak here at Vineville, I thought it would be good to give some of you the chance to contribute some thankful remembrances. I'm grateful to her and to several of you in this congregation who also just had to get it out. Some wrote, some emailed, some called me on the phone, and I called some. I'll start with one that I called.

I called Albert Reichert, Sr., as I did several more of you, to see if he'd take a part in underwriting the cost of printing the book so that all the sales could benefit the Methodist Home for Children and Youth. After graciously agreeing to help, he told me about being in college up at Emory with Frederick. He said, "He was the same then as he proved himself later to be. He was a Christian gentleman through all his fraternity and dormitory life in college. You knew then exactly how he was going to turn out—a consistent, caring, Christian character."

He also told me the amazing story of how his son picked up an old New York Times when he was up in the East somewhere. The gist of it was that in that paper was an article by some reporter who had been covering the Columbus Georgia beat during the time that Lieutenant Calley was being roundly condemned for the Mi Lai massacre during the Viet Nam war. He was sentenced to life in prison for either overseeing or condoning that slaughter on the part of American troops.

That reporter covering the story must have strayed into a church while he was in Columbus. Frederick, who was pastor at St. Paul in Columbus at the time, was being quoted in the New York Times saying that Lieutenant William Calley, like all those innocents who died in that ditch, was also one for whom Christ died. This man was a reconciler who believed in his fellow human beings and God's love for every one. With Alfred Lord Tennyson he always believed that:

Nothing walks with aimless feet
And not one life shall be destroyed
Nor cast as rubbish to the void
When God hath made the pile complete.
(Tennyson's, *In Memoriam*)

Dr. Waldo Floyd, Jr. called me to say all the adjectives that we all could affirm...He was a kind, compassionate, exceptional minister and preacher. But then he got into the personally related stuff—said his mother, who had played the organ for Frederick at Statesboro First, just "loved him to pieces." He told about that long ride over to Alabama to bury his grandmother, Waldo III's great grandmother, and what an indelible impression this man left on four generations of the same family. Waldo said, "Jesus showed through him," and if he had to describe Frederick in one word it would be "**others**."

John Batts could affirm that because when his wife, Virginia, died, Frederick was off on a vacation from his St. Paul's Church in Columbus. Somehow Martha Lawson reached him and from out of state he came back to assist Jack Key with the service. With him it was always, "Others, Lord, yes, Others."

Doris Batts remembered how she had finally gotten John to plant six magnolia trees in their yard and she was so proud of them. Just a few days later, they ran into Frederick at a social occasion and Frederick told them about how tired he was from just having raked up all the magnolia leaves in **his** yard. After telling him about her new trees and trying to stop John from smirking, she said to Frederick, "Thank you very much for sharing that information with us!" And he laughed that wonderful laugh as only Frederick could laugh.

Bebe Cook wrote about how she always called him "Saint Frederick," because when she remembers him she thinks of "love, devotion, trust, commitment, and true child of God." She said what most of us would say, "Words just can't express my true love and feelings for him."

L ouise Maxwell, with almost total recall, gave me a sermon on Zaccheus that Frederick had preached, but explained how she was able to do that. She said, "Dr. Wilson, with his great talent for dramatics, his facial expressions and his graceful movement of hands and his total persona etched a beautiful story in my mind forever." Haven't we been there?

She recalled how embarrassed she was to have to quit scraping corn and go to answer the doorbell with spattered corn all over her face. But who should she find there but Dr. Wilson grinning from ear to ear. She said, "He soon had me feeling like the corn Queen of the Day." He put her completely at ease while the drying corn on her face was giving her an automatic facial. His concluding prayer topped off the enjoyment of a great time together.

Natalie Barfield joined many others in calling him "Saint Frederick", because he was the most truly spiritual man she'd ever known. "Yet," she said, "he was never 'holier than thou' or pretentiously pious."

She said she remembers how one fledgling Associate Pastor said that no matter how hard he tried to duplicate Frederick's phrasing such as, "Again and again and again…" that he, the Associate, would always come out with "a-gin and a-gin- and a-gin…"

She said, "It wasn't just the adults who were deeply engrossed by his style and delivery. I remember two young boys (no older than eight or ten) who sat on the very front pew every Sunday morning, mesmerized by Frederick's sermons."

She said, "Frederick loved music, drama and laughter. One treasured experience occurred during my performance as Miss Hannigan in a local theatre production. I felt somewhat timorous about portraying such a mean spirited woman who was also a 'lush.' One night, as I reached for my flask, which was hidden away in my garter, I glanced into the audience, and who do I see on the second row but Frederick and Henry Kate, reeling with laughter! I was able to complete the rest of the two week run without a guilty conscience."

Frank Jones remembers all the references Frederick made in his preaching to growing up in Camilla, Georgia. He said it could have been like thirty or forty times a year. He said after sitting under his preaching for those years at Vineville, he almost felt like **he** had been born and raised in Camilla. So when he had to make a speech one time at the Camilla Rotary Club, he had a native carry him around to some of the places Frederick had mentioned. He went to the house where he grew up and remembered that Frederick one time told that while he was in college on a full scholarship at Emory Junior in Valdosta, the Bank foreclosed on that house. Those were depression years and fine families were up against it. He remembers Frederick saying to his father, "But Daddy, that's our home. The Bank can't take our home." But they did, and ever afterward that young man's heart was tendered toward all those who were experiencing hard times and misfortunes in life.

Frank went to the Camilla Methodist Church and remembered the amazing story of how many Methodist preachers came out of that church during that era alone. There was his brother John, before Frederick. He built First Methodist Tifton. He was the founding Pastor of St. Paul in Columbus that Frederick later served. John was an imposing figure of a man. Frederick was heard one time to say, "I never could understand why God made John so big and handsome, and made me so scrawny." But he would laugh as he said it. Oh, he loved his brother, John. About the time of John and Frederick there was Weyman Cleveland who served St. Luke Columbus, and Wesley Monumental, Savannah. There was Weyman's brother, Mike Cleveland, great preacher in the Florida Conference.

There was Tom Whiting who left our conference to be Pastor of Peachtree Road United Methodist Church in Atlanta. I heard Tom once tell about the source of those thirteen preachers that came out of that church. He attributed it to a little woman, a Sunday School Teacher, who had those boys in her class during their formative years. She was always surprised when they would write back to thank her for what she had meant to their lives. You know, you never know what you're doing at the time, and I don't even know her name. But don't you imagine that that name is written down in glory? Our former first lady wrote a book, It Takes a Village to Raise a Child, and Camilla, Georgia, must have been some kind of village in those days.

Jackie McNair remembered, "On Frederick's birthday in '68 or '69 (it fell on a Sunday) the choirs were scheduled to sing, and we planned a surprise for him. I had borrowed the words from one of his sentence prayers that appeared in the *Telegraph* and set them to music for the children to sing. 'Let Me Feel Joy, O Lord' was the title. Martha Lawson was in on it, of course, as she was at the organ. We could hardly wait to see Frederick's reaction. He was overcome with emotion and actually wept...you have probably seen that happen...and at the end of the service, he asked the choir to repeat the song."

When she had had a part in composing one of the Choir's offerings, Jackie said, "He made some preliminary remarks before hand which have stayed with me, about the gifts of making music. No one before or since has so truly made me feel connected to God. Frederick Wilson was that direct link!"

Now, that last memory, as beautiful and sincere as it was, brings us to what can sometimes be a problem in a church. In the ministry, following other strong

ministers is often problematic. Even the Apostle Paul had that problem. Apollos must have been some charismatic preacher, because Paul had to quell the tendency to make unflattering comparisons within his congregations. In the church at Corinth they even had groups of people who called themselves the followers of one preacher over the other. I Cor. 1:12-13 *[12]What I mean is that each of you says, 'I belong to Paul', or 'I belong to Apollos', or 'I belong to Cephas', or 'I belong to Christ.' [13]Has Christ been divided? Was Paul crucified for you? Or were you baptized in the name of Paul?* He tries to settle it by saying, (I Corinthians 3:4-7)
[4]For when one says, 'I belong to Paul', and another, 'I belong to Apollos', are you not merely human?

I shall never forget your gracious Jim Webb telling me in his self-effacing way about following Dr. King Vivian at this church. We got him out of the Louisville Conference, a really powerful preacher with a Scotch brogue like Peter Marshall. But Dr. Vivian had the tendency to go overtime. Just preached l-o-o-ong sermons. So the committee went to him and said, "Dr. Vivian, you preach really great sermons, but we'd be better served if you'd let us out on time. We'd remember so much more of what you said." Jim said that when he came following King Vivian, after a while the committee came to see **him**. They said, "Brother Jim, it's not that your sermons are so long. They just seem that way." But there's the tendency to make comparisons in negative ways.

Tom Johnson, who grew up in this church, called me last Sunday night. He told me that Dr. Leonard Cochran was appointed Pastor at Albany First to follow Frederick. After about three weeks there he got up in the pulpit on Sunday morning and he said, "Well, let me just tell you something. One lady said to me, 'You don't **hold** me like Dr. Wilson.' I told **her**, and I just want to inform **you**, I don't intend to **hold** you like Dr. Wilson."

Now this kind of thing and reaction on the part of the people was not Frederick's fault. I saw Sam and Helen Rogers at the Christian Enrichment School at Martha Bowman Church and I gave them one of the little books. I inscribed it inside, "To Helen and Sam, who had to follow Henry Kate and Frederick". Sam spotted that inscription and laughed and said, "I didn't just have to follow him. Most Sunday mornings when I got up to preach, he was sitting out there in the congregation. Talk about pressure!"

But he went on to say, "No pastor could have possibly had anybody in the congregation who was pulling for them more than Frederick. He was so gracious and supportive."

Frederick would be the last one to encourage the tendency to preacher worship. He'd be so mortified and embarrassed if he thought for a moment that such was occurring anywhere he had served. He'd be so pleased to learn that you people at Vineville have come to be able to love other preachers. He'd rejoice to learn that in some circles it's St. Elick, and of late, even

St. Marcus. And of all things, when Waldo Floyd called me, he not only recounted his memories about Frederick, but he told me a story former pastor Jim Rush had told him about two men that blessed the world that made forever an indelible impression in his heart and mind.

So Paul is right,
5 *"What then is Apollos? What is Paul? Servants through whom you came to believe, as the Lord assigned to each. [6]I planted, Apollos watered, but God gave the growth."*

How are we going to close this? Don't you suppose that God wants us to enjoy our memories, not just of Frederick, but of every person that has come our way to bless us? I think if Fred Craddock were closing this service, he'd say something like this:

"Do you have a piece of paper? Do you have a piece...? Well, use your worship bulletin. Would you write in the margin somewhere or at the bottom these words: I THANK MY GOD IN ALL MY REMEMBRANCE OF YOU. I thank my God in all my remembrance of you. And write a name. You choose the name. You remember the name. Write another name, and another name, and another name.

Have you written any names? Do you have a name or two? Keep the list. Keep the list, because to you, it's not a list. In fact, the next time you move, keep that. Even if you have to leave your car, and your television, and your furniture, and everything else, keep that with you.

In fact, when your life has ended and you leave the earth, take it with you. I know, I know. I know. When you get to the gate, St. Peter's going to say, 'Now look, you went into the world with nothing, you've got to come out of it with nothing. Now what have you got?'

And you'll say, 'Well, it's just some names.'
'Well, let me see it.'
'Well, now, it's just some names of folks I worked with and folks who helped me.'
'Well, let me see it.'
'This is just a group of people that, if it weren't for them, I'd have never made it.'
He'll say, 'I want to see it.' And you'll give it to him, and he'll smile and say, "I know all of them. In fact, on my way here to the gate I passed a group. They were painting a great big sign to hang over the street. And it said, "Welcome Home".'" (Craddock Stories, Fred B. Craddock, p. 153)

TRIBULATION
"What Troubles Have We Seen?"
By Dr. J. Frederick Wilson
John 14:18, 16:33 KJV

"In the world ye shall have tribulation: but be of good cheer; I have overcome the world."

One of Charles Wesley's Hymns with which we United Methodists begin each session of our Annual Conference begins with the first line, "And are we yet alive, and see each other's face?" And the second stanza reads like this,

> What troubles have we seen,
> What mighty conflicts passed,
> Fightings without, and fears within,
> Since we assembled last!
> (The United Methodist Hymnal, #553)

And there's not a one of us who could not take pen or pencil in hand and on a pad write down the troubles you have seen. It comes to all of us and the only thing that you can universally say about suffering is that it changes addresses. I had the privilege of going back to Camilla, the town where Henry Kate and I were born, where we lived out our youth, to preach a series of services at the church from which I left to become a Minister.

One afternoon they had nothing planned for me and so I decided to take a stroll through the little town. I chose East Broad Street where the house was located in which the four of us children were born. It became very noticeable to me as I walked along that I was thinking of the persons who "used to live in this house." A few times I realized that that family still lived there. I could recall something out of my youth, something out of my memory that happened to every family on that street that was trouble, that was heartache, and that was suffering.

Not a single one was spared. And here was an empty lot where a house had burned, and I remembered the night very well in my childhood. What troubles have we seen, what mighty conflicts passed. You can recount experiences out of your own life that you have known because they were yours to bear or because you were trying to help someone else to bear theirs.

During World War II, I was stationed for six months in Brisbane, Australia. I have carried through these decades some very dear memories of some very difficult times that I experienced. I did not have very many military funerals while I was in service as a Chaplain those four years. I was never near the battlefield. But I had a military service when I was at Brisbane. A fine young man whom I visited in the sick bay every day suddenly was diagnosed with leukemia. There had been no sign of it. When he had enlisted there was no indication of it during his training period. Now he was thousands of miles away from home and he has a desperate, desperate case of leukemia. He died and I had his service.

We were in the little village at Ipswitch, Australia. Four of our sailors got out their white uniforms. All we had to make do as a hearse was a half-ton truck and the simple casket was there. We stopped at a floral shop on our way out of the city and had a little bouquet placed there along with the American flag on top that embraced the casket. It was a beautiful spot—no complaints about that, with all the little white crosses that were dotted here and there in that lovely, lovely cemetery. I stood there at the head of that grave with those fine young sailors standing there with me and I thought that perhaps at this very hour in a little town in Iowa a mother and father were receiving the telegram telling them that their son had died in service. It was as painful and as lonely a moment as I ever imagined that I could feel. What must it be like to the father and the mother of a child thousands of miles away being buried on foreign soil and they would never ever have his body brought back home again?

I thought about it and I wrote them a long letter after I got back to the base and sent it on its way telling them every detail of what we did there at the cemetery. But trouble, trouble, trouble happened to thousands of homes in the wars in which we've been engaged through these years. How many in your lifetime has our nation been involved in during which young men and even young women, now, have given their lives on behalf of their country? So many of them never came back—never came back.

On the first Sunday that I was in Brisbane, I had my service there on the base at nine o'clock. So after it I was free to go into the city as I was longing to do so that I could find a church at which I could worship. I inquired and there was a Methodist Church right downtown in Brisbane. I took the tram or streetcar into town and was just a few minutes late arriving. As I was going up the steps to the church, the congregation was singing, "Joy to the World the Lord is Come!" It was the first Sunday in Advent, the first Sunday after Thanksgiving. And I sat down there on the steps because I was overwhelmed with homesickness for the first time, longing to be home again to be singing that song with my own church with my own family. As I went in the vestibule, a lady approached me. She said, "I believe you are new here."

I said, "Yes, I guess so. This is my first Sunday to come into town."

She said, "Well, I am here to welcome you to our church." And she said, "I want to give you a card with my name and address on it, and any afternoon that you are free I want you to feel free to come out and just be at home with us there. You'd be very welcome, and you could stay for tea." And so the first opportunity I took the tram and I arrived out at Mrs. Clark's house. It wasn't pretentious, just a modest little house. I went into the house and she welcomed me warmly. Mr. Clark was there and he joined her in the welcome.

She said to me, "Now, if you need the bathroom, it's in the back yard." She said, "We had to make a decision. It was a very serious decision—whether to put in indoor plumbing or to buy Billy a Steinway piano."

Billy was in the service of his country, also. He was a very gifted pianist. He had appeared with the Sydney Symphony. He had appeared with the Brisbane Symphony. He had concerts of his own. He was still a young man and he was sent away to Canada for basic training. He was in the Australian Air Force. Mrs. Clark said, "We went through so much getting that Steinway piano, I decided I would write the company in New York. I told them that my Billy was in Canada and if they had a mind to do it they could invite him down for a day to see the place where his piano came from." They arranged it, and she said, "It was a very wonderful day in his life."

Billy was in the first number of Australian casualties. In a flight over New Guinea, his plane was shot down and Billy was killed. There was the Steinway piano. I thought, "Well, I guess it is closed forever. I guess it will never be played again." But very shortly two service men from America came in and after them three more. And suddenly there were six of us—American service men in Mrs. Clark's house.

She said, "Now I have set the table. There are a few beans and a little bread and a little meat, but you are provided for. And if any of you can play the piano, go in and play some hymns and let's share a little bit." And this is what Mrs. Clark and Mr. Clark did with the death of Billy. They turned it into an opportunity to welcome into their simple and modest home lonely

American boys each one of whom had appeared in the vestibule of the Brisbane Methodist Church and encountered Mrs. Clark with her invitation.

Trouble... trouble... trouble. I was called one day to the hospital to be told that we'd had a birth and a death. On the same day a baby was born and had died. One of the lowest times I guess in any person's life is to stand at the graveside of a tiny little casket that contains a newborn baby that never had the opportunity to live. So at the appointed time very early in the morning, I stood there with the father and his mother and father and the couple's ten-year-old son. We stood and said our prayers and offered this little baby girl to become an angel in God's heaven. Then back to the house to stand at the bedside where lay the mother and to tell her every word that we spoke at the graveside of the little baby. The prayer that we offered I prayed again in her presence. Lonely, lonely, lonely... We looked there at the nursery, all waiting and prepared, but no baby to occupy it—trouble, trouble, trouble.

Have you been there? What a foolish question! Of course you've been there, and you've stood there, and you've shared such as a vital necessitous part of your life. And sometimes, sometimes inevitably because you are human and have a human heart and human mind, you have cried out, "Why? Why, oh God?" You are drawing near to Christ himself who on the cross, said that terrible, terrible thing that revealed his humanity as he was trying to remember that he was the divine Son of God--- *"Why, why, why have you deserted me, forgotten me?"*

But for the Christian, for you and for me, who are trying to be followers of Christ... to believe what he said and to apply what he said to our lives... the "whys" begin to be less frequently screamed out at the creator God... and we try to tune our spirits so that we are breathing in God rather than screaming out at him... because we remember precisely what Jesus said, *"In the world you... will... have tribulation."*

Who am I to think that I can escape it? Who are you to think that you might escape it when our Lord Jesus Christ said, *"You will have...* My Father did not give you the privilege of escaping all of the trials and hardships and sorrows of this life." You've wanted to say, I've wanted to say, "Why have you done this to me? I'm a minister. I've been one for forty-two years. I've tried to serve you. We've shared with you everything materially that we've had, and we've tried to be faithful in our stewardship in other ways. Why are you doing this to me?" We want to argue back.

We are not that privileged. Jesus himself was not that privileged... to escape the sorrows and the heartache and the pain and the disappointments and the deaths of this life. *"In the world you...will...have tribulation."* So we save ourselves, you and I, when we are earnestly striving to remember what he said and what he means to us... we save ourselves hours and hours of anguish because we do not beat our fists against the door of heaven wanting explanations for our cries. This is a beautiful difference between non-faith and faith, between the partial and the genuine person of faith. We don't beat our fists against the heart of God demanding to know why.

Why not me? Why not me? Why should I expect to escape? Why should I expect to be spared? Paul, that little man who was able to discern the very heart of Christ and the meaning of the cross and share it with us for the centuries, was the very ambassador of Christ. He was the first one really to go out and preach the crucified Christ. What happened to him? "Five times... five times I received thirty-nine lashes. They tied me to a post and across my fragile, bare back thirty-nine times they beat down upon me. Once they threw me into a little ditch and started throwing stones at me and they thought they had succeeded in robbing me of my life and they left me for dead. I've been shipwrecked. I've experienced every kind of human suffering that there is."

Why should I expect to escape? I guess Paul was the greatest ambassador of Christ that ever lived. Certainly he was the dominant figure in the beginnings of the church. Well, all this happened to Paul. And there was something else that bothered him apparently because he talked about it... a little bit ashamed of it in fact... and so he never really told us what he was talking about. He just called it a *thorn in the flesh,* which you know could be irritating and certainly painful also. He never said what the thorn was. He prayed to God to escape it, to have it taken out so that he would be more comfortable. God said, "Can't take it out, Paul. Can't take it out." He said, "It's in your hands and you have to bear it. You have to bear it. But I will tell you this, Paul, my grace is sufficient for you."

And that's what he says to us, "I can't shield you from suffering. There's no way I can separate you out on a little island with a precious few who never have anything but the beautiful sunshine and the glorious, glorious springtime and no tears, no tears, no tears. I can't do that for you. So whatever it is that you are called on to bear, I... will... be **with** you!" *"I will not"*, said Jesus, in that most beautiful, beautiful statement, *"I will **not** leave you comfortless. I will come to you."* And that's the difference between unfaith and faith, between the partial and the genuine—we do not feel ourselves alone. We are not alone.

"No, I can't cure your husband of that illness. No, I can't cause you to save this little house that you are about to lose. No, I can't bring your child back from death. No, I can't go out in the world and find your child that has run away from you. I can't do all these things that you are crying out for me to do, but I will be there **with** you as you go through it. You will not be alone. You will not be alone. You will not be alone." That's the glory of it. That's the glory of it.

So we learn finally, maybe in our maturing. We learn that we don't have to scream out, "Why?" to the whole boundaries of heaven. We don't have to hammer at the door of God to know why God is doing this. We've learned to say, "God, how can I use this? How can I use this to bring something good into the world?" Not why, but how, how? It's one of the great and glorious and inspiring things about being a minister that in the lives of human beings you so often see them asking this question, "How can I use this? How can I use this for my good and for the glory of God?" And these are the people who inspire us. These are the people who give us courage. These are the people who remind us of the words of Christ, *"I will not leave you comfortless."*

I've spoken often of that incident when Simon wouldn't accept the fact that Jesus was going to suffer, and Jesus said to him, *"Get thee behind me, Satan. Simon, you are Satan to me!"* But it's possible to become the very opposite of this when people have faced or are facing suffering. We can so deal with it that they say to us, "You are Christ to me!" Christ said he would not leave us comfortless, and sometimes the comfort comes from those who have come past the loneliness and the heartache of the "Why" to ask, "How? How can I use this to bless others?"

Art Linkletter is best known for his radio and television work. His love for children is evidenced through his many years of interviewing them for his television shows and through his books, "Kids Say the Darndest Things" and "The Secret World of Kids." You may have forgotten, though, that he really had a problem with his own kids.

In 1969, his daughter, Diane, committed suicide while experimenting with LSD. Ten years later, his son, Robert, was killed in a car crash. Having been plagued with misfortune, he could have succumbed to his deep guilt and depression that followed his loss, but Art committed his life to helping others avoid the same tragedies by becoming a national anti-drug spokesperson as he financed it on his own. Not, "Why, why did you let my child take her life?" but, "O God, how can I use this tragedy to bring something better into the lives of others?"

This is where you and I are; and, thank God, this is that to which we are called. Forget your whys. We don't have to ask why. We know not to ask why. Just ask "how" and you will get an answer. There are no answers to the "why" now. Maybe one day, maybe one day we'll understand. Maybe one day we'll understand, but not now—not now. But we can ask the question "how" and God has always had an answer to our hows. How can I use this? So we don't fight with God about it. We just pray that even as we wrestle with the troubles that have come our way, suffering on our particular crosses, that there is for us, as there was for him, a day of resurrection.

PRAYER

O Father God, grant that there may be for us a day of coming back to life again... a day for making the world a better place because our hearts were broken and our eyes were filled with tears. May each of us who has suffered become heir to that promise, *"In this world you will have tribulation, but be of good cheer for I have overcome the world."* In the name of the one who *"will not leave us comfortless,"* we make our prayer. Amen.

EXAMPLE
"Follow the Way"
John 14:6-12, 15:8-12, I Peter 2:21-23 (NRSV)
By Dr. J. Frederick Wilson

"Christ also suffered for you, leaving you an example, so that you should follow in his steps."

Dr. Andrew Sledd, who taught preaching at Emory, used to start his classes by quoting an ostentatious Latin phrase. When he had the rapt attention of all his young aspiring preachers, he'd say, "Young Gentlemen, that phrase from <u>Julius Caesar</u> means, 'Gaul is divided into three parts.' So it should be with every sermon that you preach." I tried that a while after I got out into churches, but one day at the dinner table Sunday afternoon, I got a phone call from one of my members. Said, "Frederick, we were sitting around the table here after dinner and none of us could remember what point two was of your sermon. We remembered point one and point three. But we just can't remember point two. Could you settle an argument that we're having here?"

My mind went completely blank, and I said to him, "I'm sorry but at the moment I can't think of it. But if you'll stay right there, I'll run over to my study and get the few notes I have there and I'll tell you."

The member said, "No, don't bother. You can just tell us the next time you see us at church."

When he hung up the phone, I thought, "If good members of my church who love preaching can't remember the three points of my sermon thirty minutes after I've delivered it, and not even I can remember them, then Dr. Sledd's soul rest in peace, but I am through with the three point sermon. I'll just try to have one point and deliver that the best I can."

One point is usually about all that I can remember. But this is a three-point sermon. And whether or not you remember it, it's my earnest prayer and hope that we'll all follow the way.

Jesus taught us how to live. We all want an example. The "Artist" on Television puts his model on the table right there in front of you so you can see it. And if he's there to tell us how he made it, all the better. We want something to follow. We want a person to follow. And how dangerous this is. The great fear that we have about our young people in this day is that they will follow the wrong person. I pray for them and I know that you pray for them. Most of us have our grandchildren that are coming along. And we want them to follow the right person—the right younger person, the right older person. How remarkable and wonderful that would be if they and we could just follow the right person. We want someone who'll be an example for us. Jesus is that example for us. And I want to say three things about him. He loved himself. He loved persons. He loved his father God.

First, he loved himself. A lot of times your mistake and mine is that we don't love ourselves. We don't follow him in loving ourselves. We don't remember as he remembered that he was God's, that he belonged to God, that he was part and parcel of God, that he was like God, that he was created, indeed, in the image of God. It wasn't a prideful thing. It was not an arrogant thing that he believed—that he loved himself. It was simply admitting, acknowledging that he was a very, very special person and he loved that. He loved being that. It was the kind of love that made him to be the person that he was. He loved himself.

He was humble. You remember that time when a person said, "Good master." Jesus interrupted him. He said, *"Don't call me good."* Can you imagine the Christ saying that? *"Don't call me good. Only my father in heaven is good."* There was humility about him—a very beautiful humility about him, but also about him a very strong feeling of his own importance. *"I am the bread of life,"* he said. *"I'm the way,"* he said. *"I am the Good Shepherd,"* he said. He said things about himself that indicate very strongly that he believed very thoroughly in himself, and he loved himself because he **could** believe in himself. And I love him for that reason.

"I am the good shepherd." "I am the bread of life." "I am the light of the world." It was always spoken in a beautiful humility, always acknowledging that he belonged to the father and that the father was in him making him what he was. But he never belittled himself. He never indicated in any way that he thought little of himself. He was proud in a beautiful and

wonderful way of who and what he was; and he wants you to be the same.

So many older adults begin to feel, "I don't matter to anyone. I can't do anything anymore. Nobody really cares for me any more. I'm just a forgotten soul. There's not much reason for me to live any longer." And we try to help and bless in our visits with them. But it's hard to overcome that. It's hard to get that out of the mind when he or she begins to feel that way. "I don't matter anymore. I don't have anything to offer anymore. I can't give anything to anybody anymore. And so God, you might as well take me out of my misery."

One of the reasons I love these church organizations like the Pacesetters and the Keenagers and even the little occasional socials that we try to have is that they attempt to get older adults out of the tendency to draw inward and belittle themselves. We see a group like the Rockers, older women with painted faces, but getting out of themselves a shuffle and a dance and a joke and a laugh and a lift of the spirits for all those who see them do their stuff. They make us believe that we can amount to something. I'm useful. I can be helpful. I can remember other people. I can reach out to other people inviting them. I am going out. I'm not to be forgotten. I'm not to be set aside. I have family and I love my family. I have children and I love my children. I love my grandchildren. No, I am not forgotten. I was made in the image of God and as long as I have breath, I will try to indicate that in my life. I will take every opportunity to do things with my hands, to do things with my voice… if nothing else just to listen and to hear someone else's cry of loneliness and respond to it on the telephone.

We don't have to do any big things. We understand that. We're not looking for our names and pictures in the paper. We can just do those little things that we can do that reach out and make a change in the lives of people—a call here, a card there, an invitation to the next occasion. There's a need for you always. Love yourself. He wants you to love yourself, not with an arrogant pride but with a beautiful humility that acknowledges that you are created in the image of God. As God's own creature he wants you to be mindful of what you can continue to contribute for him in this needy and troubled world. Believe that God loves you and follow the Christ in believing in yourself, as you love yourself.

He loved persons. You do too. He loved all persons. He did not discriminate. He didn't discriminate against women. As a matter of fact he reached out to women in a more beautiful and compassionate way than any one who had ever lived and I believe has ever lived since. She was a woman. She was a Samaritan woman, and she was not a good woman. And he spoke to her as gently and as tenderly and as compassionately and as searchingly as a man could. And his disciples when they found him there were just shocked. "Sitting on the well and talking to a woman…and she's from that Samaritan village down there. What in the world are you about?

We don't do these kinds of things! We don't mix with Samaritans. We don't have anything to do with Samaritans. There's not a single one of our women even who would speak to this woman, and yet you, a man, are talking to her?"

"But she's a child of God. She's a Child of God. And God isn't happy with the way she's living—any more than I'm happy now that I know how she's living. We need to change her We need to reach out and touch and change her." He didn't discriminate. Somehow he reached out to those who were less...who were less at the moment than they could be.

You know the man that was chained to one of the tombs out in the cemetery, and Jesus found that man. What a terrible... what a terrible sentence to impose on a man—strange in his village, doing curious things, things that weren't very nice in respectable company, something that wasn't very helpful, maybe even dangerous at times. So they said with his mind all confused that he was "possessed of demons." They didn't know Alzheimer's. They didn't know senile dementia. They didn't know schizophrenia. So they put him out in that cemetery, chained to a tombstone, thinking maybe that the fear of it all would shock him and bring him back to himself. And Jesus found that man. And you know the first thing that Jesus asked him? *"What is your name? What is your **name**? You're a person. You are a child of God. And God loves you... and I love you... and I will reach inside where those legions of demons torment you and I will ask them to leave and bring back the man that God wants you to* *be."* This is what he was constantly doing—always doing. He was reaching out in love and compassion to all of the children of God.

Have you ever wondered about the kind of conversation that might have gone on between Jesus and the soldiers that were hammering the nails into his hands? I've thought about that a thousand times. What did he say to them? I know he didn't curse them. I know he didn't revile them. I know he didn't denounce them. I wonder if he spoke compassionately to them. *"I know you don't want to do this any more than I'd like you to do it. But you're doing your job and I'm doing mine. Somehow in the mystery of God and his love for us all, you may find one day being drawn closer to Him by remembering that I was here with you."* Constantly, I believe he was constantly mindful of other people and their needs and speaking to those needs.

So he loved other people. And if you follow the way, you won't get tired of doing these things. Sitting by the telephone and calling somebody that felt forgotten before you called. Sitting for a little while by the bedside and just saying, "I love you." Don't forget. Keep loving the people that need your love so desperately. This is the Christ; and this is the example he gave us; and this is how he taught us to live.

And he loved his Father. Some nights when he was out there on the hillside forgetting that he was supposed to sleep, instead just all night talking to his Father. And that most important night when he was choosing the Twelve... out there trying to talk to his father about them. *"What do you think about Simon? What do you think about Judas? Do you think they have a chance? Do you think they'll make it finally?"* He was talking with his father about those that he was about to draw around him to be his close following who would carry on when he was no longer here to do it himself.

He loved his Father. He talked about it. He, in a very real sense, **boasted** about it. *"I love my Father, my Father loves me."* And he believed that with all of his heart. I know on the cross... I know what he said on the cross, *"My God, my God. Why hast thou forsaken me?"* He in his humanity was making words for us that you and I have spoken numbers of times, I guess. Oh, not facing a cross exactly, but undergoing a circumstance, an event, a crisis in our lives that we did not welcome, that we did not want. And we wanted to have no part in it, and it seemed that the whole world had become a dark and depressing place. "Why in the world has this happened to us?" We understand what Jesus was talking about from the cross... and all the people out there and all the ugly, horrible things they were saying and all the jabs and jibes that they were throwing at him... one of the thieves on one side making all kinds of remarks about him... and he was there by himself.

We understand that one moment in time he reached out in anguish to his father, *"Have you left me here alone. Am I to bear it all by myself?"*

But before he drew his last breath… that most beautiful, most beautiful of all prayers... *"Father, (No longer 'My God') Father, into your hands. Into your hands I commit my spirit."*

And that's finally the way you and I have to come if we follow him. Sure, we cry out in our anguish, "Why have you forsaken me? What does life amount to? What have I been trying to do all my life and now feel that I have nothing to show for it? Why are you confronting me with all of this that I don't like and don't want in my life?" Those are moments of real humanity when we cry out about being forsaken. But before our day has ended… kneeling by our bedside, lying on our pillows or sitting alone in the kitchen at the table, we speak the beautiful, beautiful, wonderful words of our Christ, *"Father, I commit it all to you. I commit me to you."*

One, he loved himself. Two, he loved other people. Three, he loved his Father God. And Jesus said, *"I am the way."* And I think it really matters to him whether we follow in his steps.

Dear Father, we so often don't follow the examples that we ought to follow. We are tempted to follow something less, something that demands so much less of us. But we love Christ. And we want to follow Jesus. And we'd like to be like him. And so often we sing it—"Lord, I want to be like Jesus…Lord I want to be like Jesus." This is our prayer, in Christ's name. Amen.

FORGIVENESS
"Forgive... As We Forgive"
Matthew 6:9-15, 18:21-22, 26:69-75, 27:3-5
By W. Hamp Watson, Jr.
(With indebtedness to J. Frederick Wilson for the approach to the subject.)

"Father, forgive them for they do not know what they are doing." (Luke 23:34)

In one of my early pastorates John Doe came to see me one Sunday night after church for counseling. He poured out a tale of his failures in life and the guilt that he felt over not being able to do more for his family. He said, "I've let them down and I've let God down." I hadn't had much experience then or I might have been more sensitive. The things he talked about didn't add up to any great sins in my estimation. I didn't really grasp the load of guilt that he must have been carrying. He seemed to respond to my listening. I thought, "This is cathartic for him. He's getting it off his chest. He'll feel better after talking with his pastor." And to be fair to myself, before he left he indicated an upswing in his mood. The last thing he said to me was, "Hamp, I think I may be able to make it." Imagine my anguish Tuesday when I got the word that Monday night he had killed himself with a gun. His family didn't even know he had a gun. His wife had gone off somewhere and alone in the wee hours of the night the load of guilt just became too much for him to bear.

Jesus came talking about forgiveness. In that prayer that he taught us to pray he said something about forgiveness. "Forgive us our sins... forgive us our trespasses as we forgive those who trespass against us." And I think Simon Peter very well may have said later to the other disciples, "Do you fellows realize that that's the only part of the prayer that he later commented on when he finished the prayer?" He didn't say anything in explanation of what he meant when he said, "Hallowed be thy name." He didn't explain what he meant by "daily bread," so scholars for centuries have been arguing over whether he meant daily rations to sustain us or whether he was referring to the "bread of that day" when the Kingdom of God would come with power. He just stopped to comment on forgiveness.

"If", said Jesus. And I think Simon Peter may very well have quoted him to the disciples. "If you do not forgive people their trespasses, then you've blocked your heart from receiving the Father's forgiveness for your trespasses." "Well," said Simon Peter, "he obviously doesn't know anything about how hard it is to forgive. If he'd been a fisherman all his life like I have, living the practical life of a fisherman he would know how hard it is to forgive. When a man finds you out at a great spot on the lake and pushes his boat in and lets his net down in territory you'd marked out to catch enough to feed your family... or if the man who comes to buy your fish refuses to give you the price that he promised... and you are treated this way, rather maltreated... and you're helpless to do anything about it because you're at the mercy of the only purchaser who can give you a deal that day without all your fish spoiling, and he knows it... if he had to face stuff like this, then he'd know how hard it is to forgive."

I think Simon Peter may have been the very one to raise these questions about forgiveness. Because I'm sure it was hard for a fisherman. When he was done wrong, and when he was cheated, to lie on his bed at night with very little in the little money sack tied to the edge of the bed, to try to think about what they had done to him **that** day; to say any kind of prayer to his God that would in any way bring in any kind of petition that God would forgive them, or that **he** would be able to forgive them for what they had done to him that day, I think it bothered Simon Peter.

Forgiveness. How can you forgive? How can you find it in your heart just to say, "It's all right that you did me that way? I don't hold it against you that you cheated me yesterday. I've forgiven you!" Now how do you say that? How can you mean it if you say it? It must have turned and tossed in his mind as he followed this strange man about, calling himself his disciple, trying to learn what he was about, trying to understand what he meant by what he was saying.

And so one day Simon Peter said to him, "Lord, how many times do you have to forgive a person? Seven times?" And I think Simon thought he was being very generous when he called the number seven. I think he thought he was being very religious, very pious, very righteous, very much like the Christ who had talked so about forgiveness when he said, "Seven times?" He was expecting the approval of his Lord, expecting him to say, "Why, Simon, you are learning in our school. You are really advancing in your spiritual development. How marvelous, Simon, that your heart is broadening in its capacity and in its ability to understand the weaknesses and frailties of other people. How wonderful that you're willing to forgive them."

Jesus didn't say anything like that. *"Seven times, Simon? No! Seventy times seven, Simon. Love doesn't count the times. Love doesn't keep score. Love doesn't run to the calendar and put little marks for the day the number of times that something was said, the number of times that something was done, the number of little slights that were made, the little omissions that showed you were forgotten. Love does not count the times, Simon, and if you love, then you don't enumerate and add up in little columns the number of times that you've forgiven anybody. It's seven times seventy! The number is endless, Simon, because love does not count the times. You keep on forgiving. This is the way God is. And if you want to be like God or if you want to open and enlarge your spirit to contain and receive some of the blessings of God's forgiveness then you've got to enlarge your own capacity to forgive or you can never receive the forgiving love of God."*

I think Simon turned away... hurt. I think he turned away resentful. "I went to him with a reasonable proposition. I approached him as a reasonable man. I figured it out in my own mind and seven is a good round number. It speaks of perfection in Jewish thought. And if I forgive a person seven times, that's just great. I would have really become a man with my spirit really standing tall. And it would show that I really understood what he was talking about when he talked about forgiving. Can you believe it that he told me, 'Not seven times, but seventy times seven?' He still doesn't know what it is to be hurt. He still doesn't know what it is to be cheated. He still doesn't know what it is to be beaten out of what you have. He still doesn't know what it is to be belittled by people. He doesn't know. He hasn't experienced what it's like to have to forgive. All he's ever done is talk about it.

It's easy enough to talk about it. Walking along the beautiful seashore or sitting again with a little group on the top of a mountain or at the center of an adoring group that surrounded you as you were performing a miracle, you're not qualified to talk glibly about forgiveness. But it's a different story when you've been slapped on the face and you stand there wondering what you're going to say… and think that you're supposed to say, 'I forgive you and I don't hold that against you.'"

So I think Jesus' response to Simon put something inside Simon that he carried with him all of their days together. He was never quite able to comprehend this. How do you forgive? How does one forgive? So that night when the soldiers came and took him in the garden and walked back through the dark and deposited him at the place where he was to be judged, Simon because there was a strong attraction inside him for this man... Simon because there was a feeling of guilt inside him because he had not really measured up to what he knew this man wanted him to be, followed at a safe distance and found himself standing around a little fire there in the courtyard.   Suddenly a little servant girl looked up into his face illuminated by the fire and said, "I saw you with that man they just brought in."

Simon was suddenly terrified at being found out, suddenly frightened to death at being identified and called out to the little maid, "No, you are wrong. I never knew this man."

"Oh yes," she said, "I'm sure. My memory is very vivid. I've seen that face. I've seen this form. I know."

"No, child, you're wrong."

Frightened inside, terrified at being identified, and maybe being carried also back into one of the chambers and being accused of God knows what else, "No, child, you must have seen someone else."

"O mister, I heard you talking and I recognized your accent and I know that you're from the same part of the country that he's from. I know I'm right. I recognized your face, I recognized your form, I recognized your accent in your voice, and you do have an association with this man."

"No child, you're wrong. And for the third time I say it. I've never known this man." And suddenly Jesus walks across a little porch being carried from one chamber to another. Simon looks up into the dim light and sees the face of his Lord. "O God, O God, I hope he knows what forgiveness is all about. I pray God that it isn't just a glib thing he talks about along lovely seashores or pleasant hillsides or in a little circle of adoring friends and admirers. I hope he knows something personal and intimate about what forgiveness is." And the Master has disappeared.

And Simon is left alone. Doubt returns again. Satan begins anew to occupy a portion of a chamber of his mind. "Well now, maybe he'll show you that he understands what it's like to be terrified, what it's like to be frightened, what it is to be hurt, because the word is that he's never coming out of here to face anything but his death. And maybe when he's there suffering at the hands of wicked and evil men he will reveal what he knows and what he feels about striking back. Then he'll know how I felt around the little fire when I found my back against the wall and had to lie in order to save my own neck."

And so, I think when they led him up the hill, Simon wasn't too far away—far enough away, but not too far away. "Now I'll hear him. Now I'll hear him. I know a thing or two about crucifixions. Never saw one before, don't particularly want to see this one, but I want to hear what he says when they start with those nails. I want to hear it. Now I'll know. Now I'll know what he really knows about forgiveness. Now I'll understand that he's human as I am human and that he has to fight back with some cry that comes from his angry lips and from his hurt and wounded heart!"

John was already up there at the top of the hill with the women. And so I think James and Simon Peter followed along. "James, listen for what he has to say. I need to know, James. It's important for me. It's very, very, important for me, James, to know what he has to say."

No words, no words, until up there on the cross the words were sounded like a solo voice from the Messiah— *"Father, forgive them, for they don't know what they're doing."* They hadn't even repented out there, not a one of them. Not a one of them was on his knees asking for forgiveness. Not a one of them was weeping tears of anguish at what he'd been a party to—to cause this innocent, pure man to die there in such a terrible manner. There was no one weeping, no one crying for his sins, no one crying on his knees, and yet he cried out to his Father God, *"Forgive them."*

"Oh James, did you hear what he said? That means that he forgave me, too, James, for the lies. *'Father, forgive them,'* that meant me too, James. He's forgiven me. James, where do you suppose Judas is? Where do you suppose Judas ran to? Do you suppose we could ever find him? Do you think there's any possibility that we could ever find Judas and tell him what I just heard this man say from the cross?"

And I think that James and Simon may have turned and started running through the streets of Jerusalem until they had run down every little narrow lane and outside the city on the other side. "Judas!

Judas! Has anybody seen Judas Iscariot?" Until at the bottom of a hill in a kind of misty darkness of a strange afternoon there was a figure hanging close to the ground but not touching it—from a tree. And they ran the faster. Simon turned the body around and looked into the face of Judas. And maybe he buried his head in the bare, naked chest of Judas. "Oh Judas, if you'd only waited. He forgave us. He forgave us. He forgave us."

Oh how I wish I had been able to communicate that to John Doe that night when he came to see me. I know that there are so many things that enter into a suicide. Sometimes when rooted in depression it could be prevented with intervention and drugs. But oh how I wish that I had said to him, "John, there's nothing you could have done or failed to do that could possibly put you beyond the reach of forgiveness like that on that cross." I even presume to hope that I who failed that night to offer it am a candidate for such forgiveness from the heart of our Father God.

For Jesus Christ who is the same yesterday, today and forever is ready to offer that same forgiveness to every one of us.

BALANCE
"Life's Beautiful Balance"
Matthew 22:34-40 (NRSV)
A funeral sermon for Dr. L. E. Brown of Vineville
United Methodist Church, Macon, Georgia
By Dr. J. Frederick Wilson

"You shall love the Lord your God with all your heart, and with all your soul, and with all your mind. This is the greatest and first commandment. And a second is like it: You shall love your neighbor as yourself."

There is a very intimate relationship among Christians that should always be present but sometimes isn't. It's because there's such an infinite variety among Christians—what kind of Christian each is and what each believes and practices in his or her life.

There are Christians who retire from the world. They live a kind of monastic life. They live in meditation and prayer. Some of them have said to me, "I'll pray for you when I'm praying." And I'm grateful for their prayers. Sometimes they slip away from the monastic life to take a part in the life around them, but most often they remain faithful to their vows and they keep a very rigid schedule in the keeping of their Christian lives. Now and again, I guess you and I envy them. We would like to draw apart ourselves and live for a little while in peace and quiet. Jesus knew the value of this. He said to his disciples one day... It had been a difficult day and no doubt some before it, "Let us go across the lake and rest for a little while."

There are activists among Christians. They believe very strongly what they believe, and they are willing to fight for it. Sometimes they are willing to kill for it, and sometimes we very wisely keep away. I remember reading the epitaph of one of the pioneers in this country, and it read something like this:

> "He killed ninety-nine Indians.
> He had hoped to make it a hundred
> When he fell asleep in Jesus."

They are strong and forceful and I guess have their place. They at least make their witness, but we wonder if it's always a Christian witness.

There are Christians who exercise their religious life by feeding themselves constantly. They meet together and they read the Scriptures and they pray for the gifts of the Spirit and they celebrate these gifts of the Spirit until sometimes they become little closely knit groups and others are not a part of these groups. They are so involved in their own spiritual development, which is enviable, but sometimes it leaves so many of us out. And as they grow closer to the Christ, they are not able to fully share their faith unless people are willing to accept it just as they present it.

There are others who are sometimes called "do-gooders" because they concentrate on their good works. Most of them are humble enough not to say, "My works are good works," but they involve themselves in humankind and they reach out to humankind to serve and to "give and give and give again what God has given" to them. But sometimes they forget that they cannot operate, that they cannot live, that they cannot do their good works on their own strength.

They give out and burn out. Sometimes they turn bitter that there is so much need all around. They resent the non-involvement of others, and sometimes, sometimes their good works fail. Somehow they do not feel underneath them the everlasting arms of God supporting them and inspiring them and continually motivating them and enabling them to do their good works. And so striving to do it in their own strength, many times they fail.

Then there are those very fortunate Christians who achieve a beautiful balance in their lives…a beautiful balance in their lives. They have a giant faith in the eternal God. They have yielded their lives to Jesus the Christ who has forgiven their sins. They keep their eyes on Him, their feet are firmly planted and their hearts are filled with the faith that God is the eternal God and Jesus Christ is His son. But then they remember very well…and they rarely if ever forget that he did say, *"Thou shalt love the Lord thy God with all of thy heart and with all of thy self*—but wait!

There is another commandment that I remind you of—That *thou shalt love thy neighbor as thy self.*" And they are like a seesaw and they must be kept balanced. And so they not only have an ebullient faith in God, but they reveal that faith in their acts of love and compassion to all around them. "Who is my neighbor, Jesus?" said the man long ago. And he told the lovely story… "Whoever needs you is your neighbor." He doesn't have to live next door. She doesn't have to live in the next house. Anywhere that you discover need—that person is your neighbor. And so they achieve in their lives this beautiful balance between their faith and their ministry. L. E. was that kind of Christian.

I thank God that we moved back to Macon in time for me to know that, to witness that, and to share that. He achieved this wonderful balance in his life—his faith in God that came from innumerable sources. His death has been very, very difficult for all of us, but I've had the opportunity to know his mother and his father, and Nancy's mother, and these three lovely children, and Nancy herself. He drew from them all his own strength, his own faith in God, and his determination to give himself…to give himself in service to that God, in service to humankind.

You will suffer a personal association that we had with Dr. Brown. In our little family, and particularly now just the two of us, we've said many times, one of the most difficult things about moving, which Methodist ministers do now and again, is giving up your doctors. And you're moving into a new town and you've got to start all over with your doctors. Coming back to Macon was a great joy because we found one or two of ours who hadn't yet retired. But our eye physician had retired. We didn't know another to whom to turn and for a while we didn't need one. That's always a safe situation to be in. But every now and then we'd say, "We need to get us an eye doctor just in case."

Well, one eye began to bother Henry Kate a little bit. Like all of us, I guess, we take advantage of our doctors and wait until things are real bad and then we go and expect them to pass the miracles. So one morning abut five o'clock she awakened me and said, "I cannot bear this pain." One eye was throbbing, throbbing. "I cannot bear this pain." And I thought, "Dear God, what shall we do? We don't have an eye doctor."

Our Father must have been listening, because into my mind came that little jingle, "Let your fingers do the walking through the yellow pages!" So I went to the directory and sat down under the light and let them walk. I was in the right column. I knew that. And I came name by name…L. E. Brown. And I called out to Henry Kate, "I know L. E. Brown. He was in the Sunday School class that I taught two Sundays ago and he and his wife sat on the front row and they spoke to me immediately after the lesson was over. I know L. E. Brown."

But it was six o'clock in the morning by then. You don't call a stranger who is a doctor, who's never had you in his office at six o'clock. "Can you wait until seven?"

"Oh," she said, "I'll try to wait 'til seven."

So at seven o'clock, with trembling fingers, I dialed the number. And he answered. That's miracle enough in itself. The doctor himself answered.

I said, "Dr. Brown, this is Frederick Wilson. You may remember me. I taught your Sunday School class a couple of Sundays ago."

"Oh, I know you," he said.

I said, "We're in trouble. My wife needs a doctor. She needs one badly."

He said, "Can you meet me at the office at once?"

"Yes, we'll be there."

And so we were there. Soon I guess his senior nurse came. He called me into the office only minutes after he had looked at Henry Kate. He said, "I'll have to operate on her."

I said, "Well, what hospital do you want me to take her to?"

"She won't need to go to a hospital," he said. "I'll do the surgery right here."

"Well, all right. I'll wait."

He said, "No, you can come with us." And I didn't know what was coming… took us to a wonderful little room with a lot of equipment and he said, "You sit right here and watch."

And he with his skillful mind and skillful hands focused the laser. I had never seen that… hardly heard of it. He focused it on that eye until there was enough room for the liquid that had been encased inside of that eye to get out. She was relieved almost immediately. The Christ touch, the healing power was right there.

And so when we arose to leave, I said, "I, I will pay at the desk."

"There is no charge."

So that was a part of his compassion. I don't believe... I know... I shall never believe that we were the only ones who were the beneficiaries of his love and care and his skillful ability and his great generosity.

Soon we got to know Nancy... not the children very well, until this crisis. And I could wish for all of you what I have experienced, and Elick and I have experienced in our association with this family in these critical days and nights—Mother and Mother and the Father and three children and then Nancy herself. And I know that none of this is accidental. It didn't just happen overnight. But something that they were giving to each other, something that they were sharing with each other, something that he was trying always to give bore fruit this week and last. And I thank God for all of you... and for him... and for him.

Jesus said, *"I was thirsty and you gave me to drink. I was hungry and you gave me food. I was a stranger and you took me in. I was sick and you visited me. I was in prison and you came unto me...Therefore, inherit the kingdom which was prepared for you from the foundation of the world. Inasmuch as you have done it one to another, you have done it unto me."*

Oh to achieve that beautiful balance in my Christian life—that vital faith in the eternal God and his goodness **and** a great, big compassionate heart to share kindness and love with all of his children.

Editor's Note: I think it's appropriate to close this message with the Physicians Prayer by William Barclay that Dr. L. E. Brown kept on his desk. It was used by a fellow physician at his funeral.

L ord Jesus, when you were on earth you healed all those who had need of healing. Help me always to remember that you have honored me by giving me the task of continuing your healing work. Give me skill in my mind, gentleness on my hands and sympathy in my heart. Help me always to remember that often when people come to me they are frightened and nervous. And help me always to try to bring to them not only healing to the bodies but also calm to their minds.

When I must tell people that there is nothing that human hands or skill can do for them, give me a wise gentleness to break the news to them. Help me never to lose the thrill of bringing new life into the world and never to become callous to the pathos of the parting of death. Give me something of your skill to heal people's diseases, to ease persons' pains, and to bring peace to troubled minds. This I ask for your love's sake. Amen.

SACRIFICE
"The Lamb of God"
John 1:28-29, Matthew 16:21-23, 27:33-37 (NRSV)
By Dr. J. Frederick Wilson

In Bethany across the Jordan where John was baptizing, the next day he saw Jesus coming toward him and declared, "Here is the Lamb of God who takes away the sin of the world!"

Y ou've crossed bridges, especially out in the country, and in all probability you've seen a little sign placed there by the Department of Transportation saying that this bridge is safe for so many tons. The designers of that bridge and the contractors that built it knew that bridge could stand only so many tons of load. So this is a warning, "Don't impose more on this bridge than you know the bridge will stand!"

The creator-designer God has provided—God has tried to provide for each and every one of us a way by which we will not impose upon our own spirits more than what God knows those spirits will withstand. And the one thing I think that God was thinking of more than any other was guilt—our guilt. We cannot bear unlimited guilt. And God says, "I know that. I created you. I designed you. I am your architect. I am the one who made you, and I know what you are and I know what you are capable of doing. And I know that you cannot bear unlimited guilt." You can bear all kinds of experiences. We can bear all kinds of feelings and emotions, but we cannot bear unlimited guilt. God knew that. God has known that from the very beginning.

I don't know that you can find anywhere in the Bible any more pitiful picture than that first family. It's described almost too vividly for us in the early chapters of Genesis. Can you imagine anything more terrible than that first man and that first woman standing at the gate expelled from their garden? The very first two to occupy the earth find their two sons on the hill, one lying dead on the ground at the other's hands. I wonder sometimes why God didn't decide that maybe it was a mistake—the whole thing—and call the whole company of heaven together and say, "What have we done wrong here? Look what I have on my hands in earth where everything is beautiful... where I said day after day... 'It is all good because I made it!'

God said, "No, I will not believe that we have failed. I will not believe it. But I must do something to try to take care of their sin and guilt." And so he did. In the Book of Leviticus, God said to his priest, "On a certain day you're to call all the people together in one place and you will tell them to assemble themselves so that they can conveniently rise from their places and come forward to where you are standing."

So the priest calls to one of his assistants and says, "You may bring the goat in now." So he brings the goat in and stands the goat in front of the priest.

And the priest says, "All you here on this side... all of you who have broken the commandments of

God... all of you who feel guilty... come and lay your hand on the head of the goat and say, 'I lay my sins on the head of the goat'... and then return to your places. And you here in this center section who know that you have not kept the commandments of God and know that you are guilty of violating them, come forward and lay your hands on the head of the goat and say, 'I leave my sins on the head of the goat'. And all you here the same until all have come."

Then the priest said to his assistant, "Now lead the goat into the wilderness. The goat will die there and when the goat dies, all your sins are also gone." Primitive? Yes. Not the kind of thing you would conduct in any of our churches today? Not the kind of thing that you and I are at all familiar with? But it's the way people thought in that long, long ago time that God was saying to them, "Forgiveness is possible for you. And when you have violated my law, when you have broken my commandments and you have not done my will, then there is a way of escape for you." And so we speak of the goat as the "scapegoat."

Now travel across the centuries and there in the temple at Jerusalem stands the priest again. At the center of it all is the altar, and on the altar is a little lamb. And in front of him there was a man and there was a woman and maybe there are several older children. And the priest finds the vital place in the little lamb's neck and comes down with the piece of steel and the blood begins to flow. The little lamb dies and the priest says to the family, "Your sins are forgiven you. Through the death of the lamb you have your salvation."

I like to think that one day early in the morning, Mary came into the room in the little house there in the village of Nazareth and shook Jesus for a moment or two until he was awake. She says, "We have a little lamb! A little lamb was born last night!"

And Joseph says, "This is the lamb that will go with us to Jerusalem for the Passover."

Mary said, "Now Jesus, Joseph and I are putting you in charge of the little lamb. When we take him to Jerusalem, he must have no blemish about him, no scratches or places where the wool is pulled. He's to be a perfect little lamb and you must take care of him. You must carefully feed him. You must watch him during the day, and if once in a while you have to bring him in out of the weather and let him sleep with you, it's all right with your father and me. Take care of our little lamb."

Eventually Joseph says, "It's time to go to Jerusalem. Is the little lamb ready?"

"Yes, the lamb is ready."

So they made their journey several days down to Jerusalem and now **they** are the family standing in front of the altar. Jesus is holding the little lamb as any child would, a pet that he loved. And the priest is reading a part of the ritual. And then he stops and asks for the reason the family is standing here.

Joseph says, "We have come to ask and pray for the forgiveness of our sins."

And the priest says, "Have you brought a sacrifice?"

"Yes, we have our little lamb."

And so the priest reads more from the ritual and then he says to Joseph, "We are ready for the lamb."

Joseph turns to Jesus and he says, "Jesus, we are ready for the lamb." And Jesus holds the little lamb even more securely.

"Jesus, we are ready for the lamb! The priest is calling for the lamb!" And very reluctantly, and very slowly, the boy hands the lamb over to Joseph. Joseph in turn hands it to the priest and the priest lays it on the altar. And from underneath he brings the sharp bladed steel and the hand and the arm come down and find the vital spot.

And Jesus cries out, "No! No! The lamb hasn't done anything wrong! The lamb doesn't deserve to die!"

"Hush, Jesus. This is for the forgiveness of our sins and the little lamb has given his life that we may be forgiven."

And I think that maybe this is one of the reasons that Jesus stayed behind—to talk to the priests about it. "I don't quite understand this! I know I've read in some of the scrolls that are there in the synagogue in Nazareth about the sacrifices, but it has never been so real to me. I want to talk about it with you." Several days he was lost there in the temple asking questions. I wonder if he asked them if it was really necessary to sacrifice this little lamb on the altar. "Couldn't there possibly be a better way?"

Jesus is called by so many beautiful names. I think he must have been pleased at the time at the things that were being said about him. He asked once, *"Whom do people say that I am?"* He was called the great teacher, the miracle worker, the Son of God, the Son of Man, Prince of Peace, the Christ, the Messiah, King of Kings and Lord of Lords. Later we've added others—the Rose of Sharon and the Lily of the Valley. But of all the names, the one that sinks in and sometimes tears a little bit at the heart are the words of John the Baptist as he saw him coming down the hill toward the river, *"Behold, the Lamb of God that takes away the sins of the world!"* Jesus must have accepted that. John repeated it again, "Behold, the Lamb of God!" Was the meaning of that sinking in with Jesus even then, at his baptism?

A little later we know it was sinking in. Remember that time when *Jesus began to show his disciples that he must go to Jerusalem and undergo great suffering?* The disciples wouldn't have anything to do with that. "You're going to Jerusalem to suffer? You know you're going to suffer? Don't go! That's the solution to that. Why go if you know you're going to suffer?" Simon who was the spokesman for all of them and saying it not once but twice and aloud, "Don't go to Jerusalem! You're doing well up here in Galilee. Everybody loves you up here. They come to the mountains in the hundreds to hear you speak. Every time you walk through one of their villages they crowd around you. They're calling out their requests for help. You never lack for invitations to have bread at someone's house or a place to rest if you need it. We are doing well in Galilee. Why don't we just stay up here? It's pleasant here."

"Get behind me, Simon. You are my Satan. You are my Satan! I will not listen to you. I have set my face to go to Jerusalem." And he did. And it happened just as he said it would. He suffered there. He suffered there! And it didn't take that little band of disciples very long to understand what that cross meant... not perfectly, I'm sure... but it didn't take them long to understand enough to know that there was some reason why he was hanging on that cross. He wasn't a guilty man. He wasn't a criminal in any sense of the word. No one really spoke anything against him that was terrible. He was just there on that cross dying. And there was a reason for that and there was a purpose for that. And it was because he was the Lamb of God being sacrificed so that all the children of God need never again sacrifice a lamb. He was God's lamb.

Paul came along with that brilliant mind of his that searched the scriptures that he knew so well, and he had to say to the people that he sought to win to Christ, *"I decided to know nothing among you except Jesus Christ, and him crucified." (I Cor. 2:2)* Paul knew that this was God's way of winning the world back to himself. Because when somebody suffers for you, you can't really bear it, can you, until somehow you express from the depths of your heart gratitude that somebody suffered in your behalf.

I often tried to give blood in the drives based in my churches—like once at Statesboro First Church I went and tried to register at the desk with one of my members. I was a pretty healthy, strong, wiry person, but she looked at my slender, weak appearing frame that you might think would blow away in a strong wind, and she said, "Are you here to get some, or give some?"

But after I retired to the old Superintendent's home on the Campus of the Methodist Home for Children, once in the night I had a terrible time. I had sense enough to know that I was losing blood, but I didn't want to admit it to Henry Kate. I felt like I would be all right and begged her not to call anybody, but I fell there in the hall and when they got me up into a chair I said, "Can't you wait until six o'clock to call somebody?" And she called Dr. Houser who had me in the hospital in less than a half-hour. Hanging above me was a bottle of blood, and after that another and after that another. I said, "O God, I don't know whose blood this is. But I want you to know, God, that I would like to find them and let them know how grateful I am that they gave their blood in my behalf." I drifted off to sleep watching the blood drip into my body. I woke up thinking about the cross and the sacrifice that Christ made for me—made for me.

Have you ever thought of Mary Magdalene at the cross? I love her because he loved her. And I love her because she stayed close by his mother that day. When the mother insisted that she must go to where the cross was, Mary Magdalene said, "Well, you will not go alone. I will go with you." She'd been possessed of demons with a life hardly worth the living and Christ came into her life and gave her something to live for. He planted some joy and gave something of himself to her, and she never got over it. She never, ever forgot it. So there she stood looking up into his face. "If you think you've failed. If you think for a moment that you've failed, look down at me. I know I'm not much to look at... not much to boast of... but you saved me... and you're giving your life for me. I believe that."

And now, falling on her knees... putting her arms around the base of the cross and just kneeling there awhile... I think maybe looking up into his face which was not difficult to see now for his head was hanging low. And all of a sudden she felt something moist on her forehead... and thinking that the rain had come again, she moved her finger across her face to wipe away the drop of water... but when she brought it down, it was a drop of blood. I don't know, but I think she might have put it to her lips as she called up to him again, "It was for me. It was for me. It was for me."

Oh my dear Christian friends, hasn't that been our word when we felt ourselves in spirit kneeling at his cross. Aren't these the words that we have formed inside our hearts or maybe even voiced with our lips...? "It was for me. It was for me. It was for me."

In the name of the Father, and of the Son, and of the Holy Spirit. Amen.

COMPASSION
"Good Friday"
By Dr. J. Frederick Wilson
John 19:23-27 NRSV

[23]*When the soldiers had crucified Jesus, they took his clothes and divided them into four parts, one for each soldier. They also took his tunic; now the tunic was seamless, woven in one piece from the top.* [24]*So they said to one another, 'Let us not tear it, but cast lots for it to see who will get it.' This was to fulfil what the scripture says,*
'They divided my clothes among themselves, and for my clothing they cast lots.'
[25]*And that is what the soldiers did.*

Meanwhile, standing near the cross of Jesus were his mother, and his mother's sister, Mary the wife of Clopas, and Mary Magdalene. [26]*When Jesus saw his mother and the disciple whom he loved standing beside her, he said to his mother, 'Woman, here is your son.'* [27]*Then he said to the disciple, 'Here is your mother.' And from that hour the disciple took her into his own home.*

There is a beautiful plaintive folk song that we do not hear very often and with which we are not very familiar. But it has a very strong and wonderful message.

I think I heard him say
When he was struggling up the hill,
I think I heard him say,

"Take my mother home."
I think I heard him say
When they were raffling off his clothes,
I think I heard him say,
"Take my mother home."

I think I heard him cry
When they were driving nails in his hands,
I think I heard him cry,
"I'll die this death on Calvary,
Never to die no more.
I think I'll die this death on Calvary,
Never to die no more."

I think I heard him say,
"**Please** take my mother home."

No one offered to take her home; and had they offered to take her home, she would never have gone until it was all at last done.

There was much conversation, I take it, in the house where Mary the mother spent the night in the home of her sister. Mary Magdalene, now the beloved friend of all the followers of the Christ, was also there. And when perhaps it was John Mark who came with the dispiriting and terrible news that he was on his way then carrying the cross to be crucified that the conversation became very urgent.

"I'm going," said Mary the mother.

"Oh no," said the sister, "you mustn't go. This is no place for you."

And young John, the beloved disciple, standing close by—the only disciple present there in the home, I take it, and certainly the only one present at the cross, "No, Mother Mary, you must not go. A crucifixion is a horrible thing to witness; and when it is your son dying there, you could hardly bear it. I advise you not to go."

"Oh I'm going. I'm going. I was there when he was born. If he is to die, I will be there when he dies."

And so the three women, and John, the beloved disciple, made their way to the hill. It is hard really to understand how Mary the mother stood there for three hours—surely sitting down sometimes on a convenient rock nearby, but never taking her eyes off his face. Now and again wandering more closely so that she could see the face more clearly, again to count the drops of blood falling from his face, coming down his feet, accompanied many of the times she went there by John who loved her and loved his Lord.

One of the most beautiful and tender moments of the three hours that they stood there and he was hanging there... "Mother, John will be your son now. John will take care of you. If ever you need anything, call on John because he will be close by enough to come to your help and aid. Mother, let John be your son now. Take John as your son."

It's hard to believe that from the lips of a man such tender, beautiful and lovely words could be spoken in this time of agony and physical suffering. But he was no ordinary man. He was a God man. He showed that he and the Father were one, for God in the most terrible, terrible hours becomes that tender, compassionate, loving and caring God and would see a mother suffering and offer solace and beautiful aid. "John, take care of my mother."

But there must have been in the heart of Mary...I cannot see it otherwise...I have stood with many mothers, my own included...I've sat with many mothers whose hearts were in anguish, whose souls were in complete darkness because of circumstances that have suddenly or gradually engulfed them. They find no strength anywhere about them for body, mind or spirit, but only enough strength to cry out, "Why?" The everlasting and eternal cry of the human heart that is surrounded by darkness, "Why?"

"It was not supposed to be this way. The angels said that he would be the Son of God—that he would be a savior. And there in that stable the night he was born came shepherds to say that an angel had revealed to them that born in that place was the Savior of the world—and it was all Good News! Any pain that I as his mother experienced was lost in all the joy of that moment that I knew that I had given birth to the Son of God. And now, there he is on a cross dying? What are you doing? Where are you? Have you forgotten him? Have you forgotten me? Have you forgotten how it was promised for centuries that he would come? And now he's dying like a criminal? Why? It was not supposed to be this way."

Now she's sitting on the rock—sister on one side and Mary Magdalene on the other. All three silent. What is there to say? There was no answer for the "Why." There seems to be absolutely no answer for the "Why."

O yes, there is an answer. "Be quiet," the angel seems to say. "Wait," the angel seems to say. "Wait, Mary. Can you wait for me, Mary?" The voice of God is clear in her spirit now, and she is beginning to understand that God has something to say to her crushed and defeated soul. And to that one there—his Son on the cross, before he breathed his last. "Wait for me, Mary."

Can you believe, Mary, that one day this cross will be the hope of the world? Can you believe that men, women, boys and girls will bow in its presence, will fall down on their knees before it, will clasp their arms around it as the only hope they have for their sinful souls? No sacrifice, no lamb, no ox— nothing on the altar adequate to take away the sense of guilt that you have when you're guilty and you know it.

Can you believe that one day, Mary, this will be the hope of the world—this cross? And it will be in gold. It will be embossed with jewels. It will be of every kind. It will be placed in the most sacred places—in places where people worship him. It will be on the tops of their churches. It will be everywhere—around their necks, on their wrists, around their ankles even. And in their pockets now and again; and as they reach in for the quarter, will rub the cross with their finger.

Can you wait for me, Mary? Wait? Can you believe that one day, Mary, you will be adored—that you will be loved, and that by some you will be worshipped as his mother—as the mother of God? Can you believe that, Mary? Will you wait for that? Wait for me, Mary. Wait. There's a miracle in this day. There is a blessed miracle in this day! One day folk will put a black cloth across that cross, but they will call it *Good* Friday. They will call it **Good** Friday. Because they waited to understand that it was through this suffering and only through this suffering that sin could be forgiven, and new hearts be born, and the world be blest. Because they could believe that even God must suffer for the sinfulness of God's world.

It's the only thing that ever will work. If your child betrays you, if your child walks out in arrogance cursing you, do you think that striking him across the back thirty-nine times will bring him back to your heart and to your home again? No! It will not. It will only drive him further away. You know that. So you won't do that. You won't do that. You know within your soul, as weak and frail as it is, if there is anything in all the world that will bring him back it's your suffering love. It is the only thing that will bring him back.

God said, "I made you. You haven't forgotten that, have you? And I made you in my image. You haven't forgotten that, have you?" So if you know in your limited wisdom that it is only suffering love that can bring the lost back to the place they belong, you must know that it is also true of God. God must suffer in order that the world may know that God loves the world. And this is why he sent him. This is why he sent him.

"Will you wait for me, Mary?"
"Yes, yes, I will wait. Yes, I will wait."
So finally she took the long linen cloth and assisted another Joseph who had come beautifully into her life at this dreadful moment of her need. And with the help of the other women she wrapped it around the now lifeless body and helped to carry it to its tomb.

When Luke concludes that beautiful gospel that he wrote about his Lord whom he loved, he begins the book of Acts. He wonderfully reminds us that in that upper room where they all waited together in great expectancy to get the strength to go out and tell the world the good news, there is Mary, the mother of the Lord. She was there, waiting. She was there waiting.

Oh dear friends, will you wait for him, too? Will you wait on him? When it is your soul that is surrounded by darkness, when it is your heart that is broken into a thousand pieces, when it is your mind that is totally saturated with the terrible circumstances that have come into your life—will you wait for him? Can you believe that one day you will look back and call it a *good* day—because it was that day that you and God together moved through that suffering out with compassionate hearts more than could have come to you any other way? Compassion always comes from our own suffering. Will you call it, waiting for it...a good day—when you and God moved out into the world to say, "It is only through suffering love, it is only through suffering love that the lost come home again?"

In the name of the Father, and of the Son, and of the Holy Spirit. Amen.

PURPOSEFUL
"Finding Meaning Again"
Ecclesiastes 2:17, Romans 8:38a, 39b
By W. Hamp Watson, Jr.

How do we make the transition from—*"So I hated life, because what is done under the sun was grievous to me; for all is vanity and a chasing after wind."*
To this—*"For I am convinced that neither death, nor life...will be able to separate us from the love of God in Christ Jesus our Lord."*?

The minister goes into the home. This minister was not I, but I had a similar experience back in Eastman, Georgia in the sixties or early seventies. He sees the picture of the young man in uniform on the table. He says, "Your son?"

"Yes."

"Is he still in the service?" And the man of the house says, "He's dead." Then he walks out into the back yard and thrusts his hands down into his pockets like he would push the bottoms out of the pockets.

The minister turns to the wife and says, "It's really hard for him, isn't it, after all this time?"

She said, "Yes, because his death in Viet Nam just made utterly no sense to him."

The minister says to her, "Well, how do you stand it?"

She said, "Well, I couldn't stand it if it didn't make some sense. I would go crazy" (From a Bible Study Fred Craddock gave at Vineville United Methodist Church in Macon, Georgia)

Recovery from loss is always delayed and at times denied if the death is seen as totally meaningless. There are no easy answers here. But the people who can somehow find a handle that will open a door to at least some meaning have the best chance to recover.

Have any of you who have ever given a dollar to any charity besides the church wondered why you are now guaranteed to receive a lifetime supply of ballpoint pens with MADD emblazoned on the side of them? It's because all charities now share their lists of donors with each other. The older mom and movie star, Geena Davis, lost her thirteen-year-old daughter. A drunk driver killed her. Geena could have lost her mind. Instead she founded MADD, Mothers Against Drunk Driving. You see Geena Davis turned her grief into fuel for a cause that's pushed legislatures to take licenses away and do something about the problem so that other mothers and fathers won't have to go through the same grief.

I was listening to one of my members, a mother who had lost her five-year-old daughter to bulbar polio. In long conversations with me she spoke through a sodden face to say that life wasn't worth living anymore. She said, "Hamp, I feel nothing for anyone anymore." But I knew she was wrong. I knew she loved my wife, Day.

So when Annual Conference time came that June, Day was pregnant with our third child and was ill. I couldn't leave her to go to conference for I had no one to turn to. This mother had resigned her job at school and had quit teaching Sunday School because she wanted no contact with any child that might remind her of her loss. She had given away all clothes and toys and had shut herself off from life. But she heard about Day's plight, and before I knew it she had shown up, pushed me off to conference, and came every afternoon to carry our help home. Then she got Susan and Wade ready for bed. She was touching children again.

This was the breakthrough. She began to teach children at Sunday School again, then back to teach children at School. She was devoting herself to children like her own whom she had lost with a new passion. After we left that pastorate, we were not too surprised to learn that she and her husband had become the parents of another beautiful baby girl.

Now I know that all such stories cannot be success stories, but even when there's no hope for anything like this, sometimes a surviving loved one can make the circumstances of the crushing death and loss into a cause that drives them. Who are the marchers that raise the most money for the American Cancer Society in the "Relay for Life"? You know. Nearly always the road to recovery starts at the corner where your loss merges with some effort to help others. The surprise destination is meaning. The move from *"I hated life"* to *"nothing will be able to separate us from love"* has begun.

SURRENDERING
"Release for Renewal"
John 20:1-18 (NRSV)
"Jesus said to her, 'Do not hold on to me...'" (17)

We shouldn't be surprised that in his resurrection appearance to Mary Magdalene, Jesus said to her, *"Do not hold on to me... Do not cling to me..."* We've discovered in the loss of our own loved ones that if we try to hold on to them like they were, that they can never be resurrected in our lives. In her great grief, suddenly seeing the vision of him there, Mary must have wanted to reach out and touch him to assure herself that he was still alive exactly as he used to be.

She must have wanted to hold on to him and keep him as he had been before. But Jesus says, "Do not cling to me. Mary, you have to face the fact that you'll never again know me as the Galilean carpenter." He says, "Let me go so that I can come back to you in another way." Mary would never again see the carpenter of Nazareth. She had best realize it and be done with it and not live in a dream world. The only way she and the disciples could hope to know him again was as risen Lord, their spiritual guide and leader. In the same way, I think Jesus would say to us, "You have to let your loved ones go so that they can come back to bless you."

But this is a very hard thing for us to do. When Jeremy Bentham died, he left his fortune to one of

London's great hospitals on whose board he had served. His will stated that his skeleton, clothed in a business suit, should be at the director's meeting table whenever the board met. For more than a hundred years the minutes read, "Jeremy Bentham—present but not voting." You have this feeling about so many who lose loved ones—they cling to them and keep them hanging around them like a skeleton in a business suit.

I knew a tragic, lovely lady whose husband died and she would not face the fact. She would do nothing that would remind her of his absence. She wouldn't touch any of his things. She wouldn't go to church because they had always gone together and this would remind her that he was gone. Her house was haunted rather than warmed by his presence.

My friend, Mack Tribble, had a Grandmother Connor that he loved dearly. He wrote this to me in a letter:

"When the news came that my Grandma Connor was dead, I didn't cry. I was going to be the strong silent type. I could take it. And I didn't cry. Brother Frank Crawley came to Forsyth for the funeral. The congregation sang 'The Old Rugged Cross.' Jenny and I drove back to Charleston. I still didn't cry.

Nearly a year later one Sunday afternoon I had weekend liberty. We came into our apartment and turned on the radio. Some choir was singing 'The Old Rugged Cross.' Then I cried. I cried and cried and cried." At last I quit clinging to the past.

Grandma Connor was dead and gone. I would never see her again as I had known her. She had gone up to her Father with her Lord.

The months wore on. She came back. Memories became blessed memories that opened up my life to know her in spirit. Now she is real to me. Now she is with me all the time. I had to cry, to mourn, to give her up, to quit clinging to her as I had known her."

When I served as a pastor in Effingham County, those old Salzburgers had a burial practice that was strange to me. At the graveside the family stayed until the very last and watched the gravediggers fill the grave back up with dirt until it formed a mound over their loved one. You could hear the thud of the dirt as it fell from the shovel onto the vault and casket. At first this repulsed me, but I came to understand that for this wise people of deep faith it was their way of saying, "Goodbye, this is final. I will hold no illusions that death has not come by trying to cover over the ugly fact with flowers."

To be sure the flowers were placed on the mound of dirt by a host of friends, but not until the family had seen that this was indeed death. They had heard Jesus say, "Do not cling to me... *Do not hold on to me...*"

We say the day dies in the west.
We say "I'm dead" when we need rest.
We say "Dead right" when we agree.
"Dead reckoning"'s a term at sea.

> And yet so hard the word to say
> When one we love has passed away,
> We try with softer phrase to gloss
> The stark reality of loss:
> As if by speaking as we do
> We'd make the crushing truth less true.
> (Source unknown after an effort to trace)

But if we are able to quit clinging, a different story can be told.

Ward Brown was the Associate Pastor at First Methodist Church, Griffin, Georgia. Commuting from school at Emory, Ward was killed in an automobile accident. He had sung "I Love Life, and I Want to Live" at a recent local community talent show. He was an only child and his parents came down from Tennessee to the Funeral in Griffin. They shed tears, but they held up well as the ministers told the story of Ward Brown and his marvelous ministry for one so young. Mr. Brown spoke quietly to some people in the church. He said, "If Ward is not all right now, then the whole universe is all wrong. But I know he is all right."

Mrs. Brown said, "We only know Ward could not be beyond God's purpose, His love, and His care." I thought of Whittier's poem:

> I know not where His islands
> Lift their fronded palms in air.
> I only know I cannot drift
> Beyond His love and care.
> (#517, 1939 Edition of The Methodist Hymnal)

They took the news of Ward's death calmly. They gave him up. They came to Griffin and shared memories of him with Ward's friends. In a simple, great service at the church, hymns were sung and his life was celebrated. Until they joined him in the Father's house, his living presence blessed their lives.

So we shouldn't be surprised that Jesus said to Mary, *"Do not hold on to me..."* None of our loved ones can come back to bless us until we stop clinging to them. But if we mourn and release them and surrender them into God's care, the morning of renewal and resurrection may come.

GLORIFICATION
"Tears Before Resurrection"
John 11:1-53

But when Jesus heard it, he said, "This illness does not lead to death; rather it is for God's Glory, so that the Son of God may be glorified through it." (11:4)

Did it puzzle you like it did me? When Mary and Martha sent to tell him that their brother Lazarus was deathly ill, why did Jesus stay two days longer at the place where he was? He didn't go running to Bethany. That seems unfeeling, uncompassionate. It must be that John, who's telling us the story, wants us to know that Jesus is in charge because God's in charge of him. He's not fazed by the corruption of death.

It's like a "brother" said of Reggie Jackson when he was in his heyday as a home run hitter, "When Reggie knocks the ball out of the park, he don't hurry. He just touches the bases." John wants us to know that Jesus can do it all. We're not to expect that "being a friend of Jesus" will resuscitate our deceased loved ones through a miracle that brings them back to us like they were. But he wants us to know that apart from God the world is a cemetery, and Jesus is the resurrection and the life. If we believe in him we can have eternal life— life that's real life, here and now, and hereafter.

No more powerful Christ is pictured anywhere else in the New Testament. He raises the dead. No matter the darkness and death of your situation, he can unbind you and let you go to new life. *"Lazarus, come out! Unbind him and let him go!"*

So it's surprising, in the heart of this story, to find the shortest verse in the Bible—*"Jesus wept."* (John 11:35) Isn't this a sign of weakness in a powerful Christ?

We can explain it by saying, "No, it's not a sign of weakness." In fact, it's the other most important thing that John wants us to know about Jesus—that he's not like the Greek god whose primary characteristic was apotheia—where we get our word "apathy," the total inability to feel any emotion whatsoever. Jesus grieved with his friends and shed tears over a lost friend he loved just like a human being—because he **was** a human being. "The Word became flesh and dwelt among us."

The Pastor of First United Methodist in Atlanta, Bob Allred, says, "One of the most precious emotional events that Jesus modeled for us was that of joining Mary and Martha and their friends in weeping at Lazarus' tomb. It was a natural human emotion and Jesus wasn't afraid to weep. After all, one of his dear friends had died...This was a highly charged moment and it would have taken a cold and distant heart to keep from breaking. Jesus still weeps with us. We can call on him "24/7"—Twenty-four hours a day, seven days a week—and He is present. The greatest miracle is not his coming to take our problems away, but to join us in the time to weep." (From a Sermon in SermonConnection.com on this text)

Jesus wasn't some ghostly visitor from outer space. We don't have a high priest who is untouched by the feelings of our infirmities, but one who in every respect is tempted like as we are. You see he became like us so that we could become like him.

O yeah! We can sing about him,

"He speaks, and listening to his voice,
New life the dead receive."

But we can also say about him,

"In every pang that rends the heart,
The man of sorrows had a part."

"Jesus wept!" So when sorrow comes, don't be ashamed of your tears, and share your tears with your friends. Jesus said, "Blessed are they that mourn for they shall be comforted." That seems to imply that unless we do mourn, we won't be comforted. "Jesus wept."

But I think there's an even deeper meaning in the fact that Jesus wept. Reading the whole story enables us to see the whole Lazarus incident as a prelude to Jesus' own death and resurrection. When Jesus tells the disciples that he's going back into Judea in order to deal with Lazarus, Thomas must have remembered that it was in Judea that they had tried to kill Jesus by stoning him. So he says to his fellow disciples, *"Let us also go, that we may die with him."* (John 11:11) And after the raising of Lazarus, which was such a dramatic sign that it couldn't be ignored, the Chief Priests and Pharisees from that day on *"took counsel how to put him to death."* (John 11:53)

J esus said, *"Where have you laid him?"* They said to him, *"Lord, come and see."* And that's when Jesus wept. And when he saw the grave of his friend Lazarus, when he came to the tomb, the Scripture says, *"He was **deeply moved.**"* The Greek word used here suggests that such deep emotion seized Jesus that an involuntary groan was wrung from his heart. That weeping, those tears, that groan reflected not only his grief over Lazarus, but the anticipation of his own upcoming death. We can take the natural passing of grandparents and even parents pretty well, but when close friends, or brothers, or sisters, or spouses, or contemporaries die, there's a different dimension. Like Jesus, we look into the grave and see a different body— our own.

- I can do my jogging,
- play my tennis,
- ride my exercise bike,
- pull my rowing machine,
- and get my oat bran by eating my Cheerios and my vitamins by eating my broccoli.

I can even go skiing down a Utah mountain like an old baldheaded fool to persuade myself that I'll never die. And I'll nearly convince myself. After all, Hamp, you're a long way from a coronary or any other seizure. But let that call come in the night that Day's brother or my sister has died. We have to get in the car or get on a plane and make that long flight or ride. And we do grieve with the survivors and for the deceased. But sometime on that pilgrimage is spent looking awkwardly into the faces of our contemporaries and wondering, "Who's next?" Could it be you? Could it be—me?

Oh, Lazarus left the tomb, but the price was that Jesus had to enter it. He said it in the next chapter. You can't give life unless you die. *"Unless a grain of wheat falls into the earth and dies, it remains alone; but if it dies, it bears much fruit."* (John 12:24)) We die to ourselves before we rise to new life. We have to lose the fear of death before we rise to new life.

When I was a boy, growing up at Baxley, I was afraid of death. Strickland's Funeral Home was on the street that ran by the railroad close to the Appling Hotel where I sold papers in the early morning, and when I walked by there, the pace of my steps noticeably increased. Later when Mama made French Nugget Candy and I sold it store to store, I had to force myself to go in there to ask Mr. Strickland if he wanted to buy some. And when he offered one day to let me go back into the inner sanctum where the bodies were embalmed, I said ungh ungh!

I was afraid of death. It was such an intruder, taking the wrong people at the wrong time. It was such an enemy:

- slipping into the nursing homes, taking grandparents,
- slipping into the hospitals, taking aunts and uncles,
- putting on muddy boots, going down the center lane of the highway, snatching our friends from broken glass and twisted steel,
- putting on soft shoes and slipping into the nursery and snuffing out the breath of a little child.

And after I lost my mother to cancer when I was sixteen, I couldn't imagine death ever being anything but an enemy. I certainly never dreamed that death could be a friend.

Fred Craddock tells about meeting someone who changed his heart and mind about death. "Her name was Mrs. Gang. She lived at Crab Orchard, Tennessee. She had already died and was alive again. She had walked out to the limit, curled her toes over the edge, felt the mist in her face and the frog in her throat, and then she had walked back and she was at peace and totally free. Oh, we were worried about her. We sat up with her that last night. We knew that it was the end of her illness. And it was the custom there at Crab Orchard to sit up with the dying, and so we did.

About a quarter to ten that night she sat up and said, 'Open the door and let him in.'
What are you talking about?
'Let him in.'
Who?
'Let Death in.'

What? We're not going to do it. That's why we're here. We're taking turns holding the door so he can't get in. I saw him sitting on the ground out there with his yellow face, grinning and wanting to get in. We're...

She said, 'Let him in.'

We let him in. And I've never seen such a pitiful thing in my life as death, standing there shuffling, one foot and then the other. And I said, 'Where are your friends, pain and fear and loneliness?'

And he said, 'They didn't come this time.'

And I said, 'Why didn't they come?'

'Well, they didn't belong here.'

'Why?'

'Because I'm on a mission of mercy.'

I never felt so sorry for anybody in my life as I did for old death—robbed of all his arrogance. And then I knew—sometimes death can be a friend."

(Taken from #18 Southern Folk Advent, Meridian Herald presentation, Old Church, Oxford, Ga., Dec. 4, 1999, Recorded live, used by permission)

So Jesus wept. Aren't we glad that he wept? For tears come before resurrection. The cross comes before the empty tomb. Above all the other worship services in the church, when we celebrate the Lord's Supper, it's then that we celebrate the death and resurrection of Jesus. So when your church offers it, go and die to yourself so that you can rise to new life with him. "For as often as you eat this bread and drink this cup, you proclaim the Lord's death until he comes!"

JUSTIFICATION
"Living Like God is For Us"
Genesis 22:16-17, Romans 8:31b-39, John 8:7b-11
By Hamp Watson
"If God is for us, who is against us?"

Paul implies that the Christian life style should be one lived in the light of the fact that God is for us. Across the centuries of the Christian Faith this has been an assertion that has been subject to great misunderstandings.

For instance, you could think that Paul was saying that God will always be on the side of the Christian to make him or her win out in competitive success or failure. Often when I'm playing doubles tennis, I'll accidentally hit a ball in such a way that it will tip the top of the net and fall over dead on the opponent's side. My doubles partner will say, "It pays to be on the side of the preacher." He's jokingly inferring that the Christian has a hot line to God to help him out competitively.

I'll never forget the story of the Methodist preacher and the Catholic priest who were out playing golf. The preacher held his own with the priest until they got on the greens and then he noticed that after he missed his putt the priest would cross himself, say a prayer and then sink his putt for a birdie. After a while the Methodist preacher was falling so far behind that he began crossing himself and saying a prayer before he putted. But his ball would still fail to fall in the hole.

When they got back to the club house, the preacher asked the priest, "Why is it that your ball always fell in the hole after you crossed yourself and prayed and mine didn't?"

The priest said, "It's simple. You can't putt." Competitive success in the sports arena or the scholastic or business world can't be achieved merely by relying on the fact that God is for us.

Another misunderstanding is the feeling that if God is for us, he'll always heal us or preserve us from any physical harm in this world. There are branches of the Christian Faith that major on "praising the Lord" and "healing" only. While these should certainly be included in any mature faith, the end result is often to leave out the cross and redemptive suffering as a part of the Christian's life. Paul said, "I am determined to know nothing among you save Jesus Christ and him crucified." He said that he completed in his body what was lacking in the afflictions of Christ for Christ's sake and the sake of the church. But some of the electronic priests would have us believe that the Christian life consists of just praising the Lord and praying for healing. You can stretch out in front of the television and send in a dollar now and then and all will be rosy and right in your life from now on. They forget that the heart of the gospel is the cross and that there's a cost to discipleship. This can lead to great distortions.

I became deeply concerned for a dear friend of mine who lost his wife with cerebral cancer. Ten years earlier she'd had brain surgery to remove a tumor and though the chances were very slim, she miraculously recovered living ten more years gratefully and graciously. She blessed the lives of all that knew her by her attitude in suffering. But in the last stages of this illness that finally killed her, a group of friends that were in a healing prayer group came to both her and her husband with the implied message that they just didn't have enough faith or the wife would be healed.

When she was dead they were still dogging the husband with this half-baked, misguided theology. Forgetting the lifetime of service of this man in his church in every large or small office he could hold, forgetting the miracle of her first deliverance from death and the bonus of ten more happy years, these misguided people were still hovering around the corpse to claim another victim. I wanted to cry out to them, "Get off this good man's back and let him live with the memory of a living presence. Let him live with the memory of a courageous, precious lady who blessed all who knew her because she knew that whether she lived or died she was the Lord's." The fact that God is for us doesn't preserve us from all physical harms in this world.

This doesn't mean that God is not for us. Paul uses the strongest language that he can to convince us that God does love us and is supremely for us. He says, *"He who did not spare his own Son but gave him up for us all, will he not also give us all things with him?"* (Romans 8:32) In the reading from Genesis this same language is used by God in talking about Abraham. For God, it's the proof of Abraham's complete loyalty to him that he would not withhold his son, his only son, Isaac, from him. Paul picks up on this and seems to say, "Think of the greatest human example in the world of a person's loyalty to God. God's loyalty to you Christians is like that." Just as Abraham was so loyal to God that he was prepared to sacrifice his dearest possession, God is so loyal to us that he **did** give up his only son for us. Surely we can trust a loyalty like that for anything. So God loves us. God is for us! There's no question about it.

Then what's involved in living like God is for us? For one thing, it's LIVING FREE FROM CONDEMNATION—free from our burden of guilt and self-despising. In the imagery of the courtroom Paul waxes eloquently, "Who shall bring any charge against God's elect? It's God who justifies. Who is to condemn? Is it Christ Jesus, who died, yes, who was raised from the dead, who is at the right hand of God, who indeed intercedes for us?" I run into Christians sometimes who in spite of all their church going, praying and Bible reading seem unable to accept the fact that they are free of their load of guilt for past sins or present imagined violations. I know preachers, including me, that live at times as if we were tried before the judgment seat of God tomorrow we would be condemned and thrown under the jail, locked in and the key thrown away. So much can we condemn and despise ourselves sometimes.

Paul says that the Christian doesn't have to live like that. You think of Jesus as the judge who is there to condemn. Oh he has the right to, in view of what we have been and are, and in view of the life he lived. But you are wrong. He's not there at the right hand of God to be the prosecuting attorney, but to be the advocate to plead our cause. He's our Perry Mason. He's our Matlock. And the judge himself, God, sent him to do it. He's our court-appointed attorney, in our behalf, appointed by God himself. God is for us. He and Christ are lovers of the souls of people like you and me.

So we can sing the old children's chorus,

For there is therefore now no condemnation down in my heart,
Down in my heart, down in my heart.
For there is therefore now no condemnation down in my heart,
Down in my heart to stay."

No need to go around guilt ridden. If God acquits you then you are saved from every other condemnation. Living like God is for us is living free from condemnation—free of our own guilt and self-despising.

The next thing follows naturally. Living like God is for us is LIVING FREE TO FOLLOW JESUS. We are freed from the compulsive patterns of the past once we recognize that we are no longer condemned for them and condemned to remain in them. This is the significance of Jesus' words in that powerful incident when he spoke to the woman caught in the act of adultery. Those who would have cast stones have slunk away in the knowledge of their own sin and Jesus looked up and said to her, (John 8:10) *"Woman, where are they? Has no one condemned you?"*

She said, "No one, Lord."

And Jesus said, "Neither do I condemn you; go and do not sin again."

No matter who we are and what we have done, we are free to go and not sin again once we realize we're not condemned. It's like hitting the undo button on the computer. We can start a new line of type. If the slate is wiped clean, we can start writing a new story on the blackboard of life. In Columbus, Georgia an alcoholic named Roy K said to a reformed alcoholic Judge who was working with him, "God can't possibly forgive me." He was thinking of how he had messed up his family's life through his addiction. "God can't possibly forgive me!"

The judge said to him, "Well you must think you're better than God."

Roy said, "Oh no, I don't think that."

The judge said, "You must, because if you had a son and he was repentant of his wrong doing and was willing to change his life, you'd forgive him wouldn't you?"

Roy said, "Yes."

The judge said, "Well then you're not better than God and more loving than God. How can you presume that God is not as much for you as you would be for your son?"

God is for us, and since we are no longer condemned we are freed from the compulsive patterns of the past. If we think we're hopelessly condemned alcoholics, adding one or two more drinks won't make any difference. There's nobody that's such a compulsive spender as the person so hopelessly in debt he knows he can never get out. Why not spend some more—write another check even if there's nothing to cover it just for the kicks of the moment? Use that charge card one more time! But if the debt is cancelled, if the sin is forgiven, we just might be able to put our house of life in order and start over. *"Neither do I condemn thee. Go and sin no more."* Living like God is for us is living free to follow Jesus—freed from the compulsive patterns of the past. That's good news!

Now Paul becomes explosive in his poetic language when he tells us that living like God is for us is LIVING FREE FROM FEAR OF ANY KIND. Ro. 8:35 *"Who shall separate us from the love of Christ? Shall tribulation or distress or persecution or famine, or nakedness or peril or sword? It is written, 'For thy sake we are being killed all the day long.' No, in all these things we are more than conquerors through him who loved us."* When we take the view that we go through these things for God's sake and Christ's sake, then no affliction, hardship or peril can separate us from the love of God in Christ. They only serve to bring him closer.

In the list of these things is famine—going hungry. Everybody today is concerned about corporate and accounting embezzlement of stockholders value. Paul might well have put that on his list for it might lead to famine for some of us who are dependent on fixed income and savings. But we have no fear of this.

Paul says, *"For I am sure that neither death nor life"*—no fear there, for in this perspective, death is just a gate on the skyline leading into the presence of Christ.

Paul says, *"Nor angels, nor principalities"*— These angelic powers can't separate us from God. When Paul wrote this the Jews had a highly developed belief in angels. The rabbis believed that angels were grudgingly hostile to people. They believed that the angels got angry when God created humans. It was as if they didn't want to share God with anyone. So Paul says not even the grudging, jealous, powerful angels can separate us from the love of God as much as they would like to do so.

Paul says, *"Nor things present, nor things to come."* He's already told us not to be shackled by the past. Now he says don't be afraid of the present or the future if God is for us—not what Osama Bin Laden or Al Queda **are** doing or even what they **might** do. Emerson said, "All that I have seen causes me to trust God for all that I have not seen."

Paul says, *"Nor powers nor height nor depth"*— These are astrological terms. The ancient world was haunted by the tyranny of the stars. They believed that a man or woman was born under a certain star and thereby their destiny was settled. There are some that still believe that or play at it as they follow their daily horoscope in the newspaper. But the ancient world was really haunted by this supposed domination or your life by the influence of the stars.

Height or "hup soma" was the time when a star was at its zenith and its influence was the greatest. Depth or "hathos" was the time when a star was at its lowest preparing to rise and pounce and put its influence on some unsuspecting person. Paul said to the haunted people of his age, "The stars can't hurt you. In their rising and their setting they are powerless to separate you from God's love." Do you meet people who seem haunted by a sense that fate has already written their dark story? Have you ever felt that way? Paul says that if you're a Christian, don't. God is for us.

Paul says, *"Nor anything else in all creation will be able to separate us from the love of God in Christ Jesus our Lord."* What about "Star Wars" and E.T.— extra terrestrial beings? What if we do discover other worlds that don't know Jewish history or Christ at the center of our history? Paul says don't be afraid of other worlds or other world creatures. Even if they don't know about Christ, the love that created Christ created all worlds that are and all that are to be.

> "I know not where his islands lift their fronded palms in air.
>
> I only know I cannot drift beyond his love and care." (Whittier)

Think of every terrifying thing that this or any other world can produce. Not one of them is able to separate the Christian from the love of God, which is in Christ Jesus our Lord. Of whom then shall we be afraid?

It can make a powerful difference in your life if you ever once realize that God is really for you. Roy Smith grew up out on the plains of Kansas when times were very hard. His father worked in the mill— never made more than a few dollars a week. Roy said it was hard for his parents to scrape up enough money for him to go to college, but he wanted to go to the little Methodist College in his hometown. Somehow or other his parents managed to get him enrolled.

Then Roy was given a part in a debate that would put him on stage. More than anything else in the world he wanted a new pair of shoes for the big day. Somehow, out of their meager income, his parents managed to buy some new shoes for their son. Just before Roy went on stage, someone burst through the doors of the auditorium and shocked him with the news that his father had been hurt badly in an accident at the mill.

Roy ran down the streets of that little town into the mill, but it was too late. His father had died. They buried him the next day—a cold and windy afternoon. And then Roy went back to the mill to get his fathers tools and the coveralls that he had been wearing at the time of the accident. Someone had thoughtfully put them all into the toolbox his father had used. They had carefully folded the bloody coveralls and then had placed his old brogans bottom side up there in the box.

When Roy Smith opened the lid of that box the first thing he saw was his father's shoes. Those shoes had holes in the bottom that stretched from side to side. In that second, he realized that while he stood on the stage in his new shoes his father had stood on the cold steel of that mill floor in shoes that didn't protect his feet. Roy Smith never walked in his new shoes again without remembering how much his father was for him.

> "I gotta shoes. You gotta shoes.
> All of God's chillun' gotta shoes.
> When I get to heaven gonna put on my shoes—
> Gonna walk all over God's Heaven!"
> (Spiritual)

We don't have to wait until we get to heaven. We can boldly face the worst that the world can throw at us LIVING LIKE GOD IS FOR US!

ACCEPTANCE
"I Don't Want to Talk About It"
Mark 8:31-33

"Then he began to teach them that the Son of Man must undergo great suffering...and be killed...and Peter...began to rebuke him."

When I was buying our family's plane tickets to fly out to ski this winter, Day said, "Please, don't all of you go on the same plane. I couldn't stand it if I lost all of you at once." When I told my son and daughter about it—same reaction from both. "Daddy, don't talk like that! Don't even talk about it!" We did talk about it and we did take separate flights.

When Jesus said, "I'm going to die," Peter rebuked him. This most human of the disciples, Peter, reflected our common reaction when we hear the announcement that anyone is going to die. We are repelled by it. "I don't want to talk about it." Peter probably scolded Jesus for even talking as though he wouldn't always be with them just as he was then.

In a 600-bed hospital I know about, the staff wouldn't admit they had a patient that was going to die. Yet seventy-five to eighty percent of the nation's deaths take place in an institution. Isn't this strange?

Just as Jesus wanted to talk about his coming death with his disciples, so people who have terminal illnesses need to talk about their coming death and come to some resolution of it in their minds. They need the support of those who are close to them to share the meaning of this experience with them. But the disciples didn't want to talk about it even in the Garden of Gethsemane. Jesus says, (Mark 14:34ff.)

> *"My soul is sorrowful unto death. Stop here and stay awake with me." He went on a little, fell on his face in prayer, and said, "My Father, if it's possible, let this cup pass me by. Yet not as I will, but as you will." He came to his disciples and found them asleep.* (That's avoiding it about as far as you can, isn't it?) And he said to Peter, *"What! Could none of you stay awake with me one hour?"*

Just like the disciples, a lot of us today seem to be conspiring to abandon people to face the drear prospect of death alone.

The reason it's so rampant in adult life is because we start early training little children that death isn't a topic that adults can discuss comfortably. There was a day when children were allowed to stay at home and be included in the talk when loved ones were lost and it gave them the feeling that they weren't alone in their grief. It prepared them gradually and helped them view death as part of life, an experience that helped them grow and mature and come to recognize their own finite nature. "As this person died, I too will one day die."

One of the favorite stories in my wife's family is about a little red-headed fellow named "Sonny" asking his grandma who built the house they lived in.

She said, "Your great-grandfather Gwynn."

Sonny said, "Well, where is he now?"

Quite naturally she said, "He's dead."

Sonny said, "Well, who stepped on him?"

Killing bugs by stepping on them had been his only experience of death. And from that, his grandmother led him into a healthy discussion about how all living things will one-day die, not necessarily by being stepped on.

This is in great contrast to us today, when death is viewed as taboo, discussion of it is regarded as morbid, and children are excluded with the presumption that it would be "too much" for them. They're then sent off to relatives, often accompanied with some unconvincing lies such as, "Mother has gone off on a long trip," or other unbelievable stories. The child senses that something is wrong, and distrust of adults will only multiply if other relatives add new variations of the story, avoid his questions or suspicions, and shower him with gifts as a meager substitute for a loss he's not permitted to deal with.

Sooner or later the child will become aware of the changed family situation, and depending on the age and personality of the child, will have unresolved grief and regard this incident as a frightening, mysterious, traumatic experience with untrustworthy grownups that he has no way to cope with. Schooled in this kind of world, no wonder when the child grows up and becomes us, we're still afraid to talk about death.

Our faith makes no such mistake. Death in the scriptures is treated as a natural part of life. Though we can't buy its fatalism, we have to recognize the wisdom of Ecclesiastes 3:1-4—

> *"For everything there is a season,*
> *And time for every matter under heaven:*
> *A time to be born, and a time to die;*
> *A time to plant and a time to uproot;*
> *A time to kill and a time to heal;*
> *A time to pull down and a time to build up;*
> *A time to weep and a time to laugh;*
> *A time for mourning and a time for dancing."*

Wise people, in accepting the shining side of life, will also anticipate the inevitability of its shadows—a time to be born and a time to die.

"I don't want to talk about it." And because I don't, and won't, I may wind up being as cruel as those disciples were who wouldn't even talk with Jesus about his impending death. At old Candler Hospital in Savannah I heard Dr. Elizabeth Kubler-Ross say that even little children that are facing death have a desperate need to talk about it. She said they'd do it with symbolic, non-verbal language if they couldn't yet put it in plain English. She told about a little eight-year-old boy that had an inoperable brain tumor. Nobody knew that he knew it, for he hadn't been told.

He was given some artwork to do and the first picture he drew was of a pretty little house in the background with some trees, flowers and sunshine. But in the foreground was a huge tank. Suspended in front of the gun of the tank where the shell comes out was the tiny figure of a boy with a stop sign in his hand. Dr. Ross had earlier explained that the fear of death is the "fear of a catastrophic destructive force bearing upon me and I can't do a thing about it."

She said, "If this little boy gave you this picture, it would mean he had chosen you to talk with about his impending death."

She took the picture and said to him, "It must be terrible to feel so tiny when the tank is so big." When she said that, the little boy poured out his fear and anger and depression and sadness. He talked it out in that session and several more sessions that he had with Dr. Ross.

Sometime later he drew another picture. This one was black and white of a flying bird with the tiny part of an upper wing painted gold. She said, "Tell me about this."

He said, "Naturally, this is the peace bird flying up into the sky with a little bit of sunshine on **MY** wing."

This was the last picture he drew before he died.

"I don't want to talk about it." But if I can overcome my reservations, maybe I can help somebody move from the concept of dying as a catastrophic destructive force. I might even move from my fear and anger and depression and bargaining phases until I come to a final stage of acceptance and hope. I might come close to somebody and share their sorrow with them and help them through it. When friends get the word that they have a terminal illness or they suspect it, we wouldn't then avoid them and find excuses not to go to their homes or their hospital rooms. As the family of God we might be able to go do what we could and to listen and be taught about death by the dying patient. We'd learn something about our own fears of death and overcome them.

Oh, we need to be cheerful. Humor is always needed in a sickroom. And we need to hold out hope in the early stages for cure, for treatment, for possible prolongation of life. But when this is no longer probable, (Now I didn't say, "When this is no longer **possible**,") but when it's no longer probable that they can get well, trust that the patient and maybe we, ourselves, will develop that other kind of hope which says something like,

- "I hope my children are going to make it," or,
- "I hope God will accept me in his Garden," or,
- "I'm ready to go."

"For me to live is Christ and to die is gain." (Philippians 1:21)

But that doesn't mean we want to rush up the process. The oldest church joke around that came out of Noah's Ark on crutches makes the point. One night at church the Preacher says, "Everybody that wants to go to heaven, stand up!" Everybody stands up but one old man in the back.

"Don't you want to go to heaven when you die?" Old man says, "Sure, but I thought you were getting up a load for tonight."

I know it's natural for us not to want to speak of death. One of my favorite little snatches of poetry from Jane Merchant says,

"We will not speak of separation while the frail hours grow less.
Nothing shall mar the perfection of our togetherness."

We'd be morbid if we longed for death and just wanted to talk about it all the time. But there comes a time when not to speak of death and to listen to those who want to talk about it is cruel. Paul said, *"Rejoice with those who rejoice,"* but he also said, *"Weep with those who weep."*

The Puritans had a prayer they used to pray, "Lord, give us the gift of tears."

We can sometimes see farther through a teardrop than we can through a telescope.

A need shared is a need halved, so we bear one another's burden and thus fulfill the law of Christ.

As unnatural as it seems to us, we Christians find the courage to talk about death and face it with our friends and loved ones because nobody has a greater faith than ours to deal with the final hope. Paul put it, *"Whether we live or die, we belong to the Lord."* (Romans 14:9)

A young woman with a terminal illness was planning her funeral with her minister. They'd picked out the songs, talked about the order of service, the scriptures, and he was about to leave when she said, "Oh I almost forgot. Please ask the funeral director to put a fork in my right hand."

Minister said, "I can do that, but why?"

She said, "When I went to my grandmother's house as a child, when we finished the meal, she'd always say, 'Keep your fork.' I knew that meant that chocolate cake or deep pan apple pie was coming. Something wonderful and of deep substance was yet to come. So at the funeral, if people are thinking, 'What's with the fork?' you can tell them all to keep their fork. The best is yet to be." (Circulating on the Internet from an anonymous source)

We can't answer all the questions about death. Even our Lord said, *"My God, My God, why hast thou forsaken me?"* But he moved through the experience of death to the point where he could say, *"Father, into thy hands I commit my spirit."*

"I don't want to talk about it!" But God, help me move from being repelled by the death announcement to the final stage of acceptance and hope. And if we have loved ones and friends who are dying, God grant that through our sharing and caring they may get a glimpse of the peace bird flying up into the sky with a little glint of sunlight on its wing.

TRANSFORMATION
"When Trouble Troubles You"
Romans 15:14-29, 8:26-30 (NRSV)

*You have seen... how I bore you on eagles' wings
and brought you to myself. (Exodus 19:4 NRSV)*

My mother used to say to me when I was a boy, "Don't trouble trouble, until trouble troubles you." Across the years I've lived since then, I think I've learned that. I know not to go out and seek trouble, to live in such a foolhardy way that I stir up trouble or suffering for myself or those I love. But after she died of a double mastectomy at the age of 48, I've longed to be able to bring her back to ask her, "But what do you do when trouble troubles you?" What do you do when suffering or trouble comes your way when you didn't ask for it or provoke it or even anticipate it?

The life of St. Paul, the Apostle, was stalked by trouble. His life was different from the life of a minister today. The modern preacher expects a **good** appointment after serving a church well, but Paul found only **dis**appointment. He seldom shifted from one church to a higher paying church. The best he could hope for was changing from a bad jail cell to one a little bit better. We expect pensions at the end of our lives, but Paul found a prison at the end of his. When Paul went to preach in a town it wasn't just a few smooth services, they either had a revival or a riot, and more often it was the latter with Paul the one who was being run out of town—barely escaping the clutches of an angry mob. All through his ministry he was tormented by what he called a "thorn in the flesh", some sort of intense physical trouble or illness. (II Cor. 12:7)

One of the saddest defeats of his ministry is recorded in a little sentence that he includes when writing to the Church at Rome. Trying to enlist their loyalty and support for his future mission to the farthest reaches of the known world at that time, he says to them, *"I desire, as I have for many years, to come to you when I go to Spain. For I do hope to see you on my journey and to be sent on by you, once I have enjoyed your company for a little while."* (Romans 15:23b-24, NRSV)

When he writes this letter, Paul intends to carry the gospel into Spain, and to use the Church at Rome as a base for his operations. He wants to go to Spain, he has his heart set on it and he has a great dream of Christian conquest there. But Paul never reaches Spain. Instead of using Rome as a base to carry the good news of Christ to that land, Paul gets a prison cell in Rome. There he sits now, rotting his life away in a prison, scribbling on a little bit of parchment.

I think one of the biggest roots of all the mental illness and despair of our generation is the fact that people have only been trained for success, but few have been trained to meet failure. Never having come to grips with the problem of trouble and pain and defeat, many find themselves stymied by it. Turning to first one solution and then another but never finding the answer of faith, they come up against a brick wall with no help and no hope. So what do you do when trouble troubles you?

You can resent it. You can start out with the idea that the ideal life is the unruffled life and that the providence of God means security and protection from all trouble. And when that doesn't happen, when the formula doesn't work you can resist it and resent it. You can be baffled by it so you never find your way out of it.

The students in that Air Force class were all trying to talk at once. They were all hopping their instructor for one particular problem he had put on their final exam. They asked him all kinds of questions about it and complained of its even being on the test. Then the instructor turned to them and said, "Don't F.T.P." They all smiled because they all knew what he meant. It was classroom slang for what he had said to them a hundred times. Don't fight the problem. Don't FTP. Quit letting it scare you, quit resenting it, quit asking so many questions and go to work on it.

They did settle down and most of them found that they could find the answer to the hard problem.

Day's brother, Farris, was a chemist for Goodyear. He said that they tried at first to make a tire that would resist the shocks of the road. It was a tire that was soon cut to pieces. Then they started making tires that would give a little and absorb the shocks. Those tires are still with us. They are enduring because they are resilient. They have bounce-back power. They face strain and stress the way we should begin to. Not resisting or resenting they roll with the punches and come back up to roll for many more miles.

Some get caught in the grip of the "iffing" reaction to trouble, and before long it turns into self-pity. They say, "If I hadn't done so-and-so maybe things wouldn't have happened as they did and I wouldn't be in this mess now." They relive a whole life "iffing" their way through it and feeling sorry for themselves because destiny has treated them as it has.

Can you imagine Paul doing this? Rotting in prison he says, "Oh **if** I had only been able to go to Spain, I would have carried the gospel all over the world." Or, "**If** I had just not followed this Christ, I wouldn't have gotten into this terrible situation. **If** I hadn't, today I would be a great Rabbi. I would be saluted in the marketplace. **If** I had just watched myself more carefully and spared myself because of my weak physical condition, I never would have come to this place." Would he be "Saint" Paul? Have you ever seen a happy "iffer"? Unless it can be stopped, it will turn into self-pity and the person will be found feeding on the rancid food of a sour and sullen mind.

What do you do when trouble troubles you? The turtle has a way. You can take life's disturbances and disappointments like the turtle takes the prodding of stick. You can't hurt a turtle very much by knocking on its shell. We can make a shell, too. We can take whatever comes and get pretty hard and callused in the process. One turtle shell is saying to ourselves that all things that happen are good. We can resign ourselves to whatever comes, and blindly accept it as fate. We can pull the wool over our eyes by saying this is the best of all possible worlds, and all things that happen are good. God never said this. The devil causes some things. In the Bible God recognizes some things as terrible and through Christ tries to get rid of them. Paul never said that all things that happen are good. He says that his thorn in the flesh is *"the messenger of Satan to buffet me." (II Cor. 12:7)*

L in Yutang tells the ancient Chinese parable about the old man who lived with his son in an abandoned fort. One night the old man's horse—the only horse he had—wandered away, and his neighbors all came to say how sorry they were about his misfortune. He said, "How do you know this is ill fortune?"

A week later the horse came home, bringing with him a whole herd of wild horses. The neighbors came again, helped him capture the wild horses, and congratulated him on his good fortune. The old man said, "How do you know this is good fortune?"

As the days went on the old man's son took to riding the horses. One day he was thrown and wound up with a crippled leg. The neighbors appeared again as if they had been hanging behind the old man's shoulder, to tell him how sorry they were about his back luck, but the old man said, "How do you know it is bad luck?"

In less than a week, along came a Chinese War Lord conscripting all able-bodied men for his private little war, but the old man's son being a cripple, missed the draft. Once more came the neighbors to rejoice with him in his good luck, and again the old man said, "How do you know this is good luck?"

The story ends there but it could go on forever. This never calls evil and troubles what they are—evil! It passively, fatalistically takes what comes, never doing anything about it. Like a turtle it goes plodding on, covered up in a shell, enduring life. I have a picture of that old man in my mind. His face is stolid, immobile, and joyless.

We can get a partial answer to the problem of trouble by compensating when it hits us. In 1915 the boll weevil had almost put Coffee County Alabama out of business. But then a white-haired Negro scientist named George Washington Carver came along and started the people to growing peanuts to take the place of the destroyed cotton crop. He found "I don't know what all" in the peanut—chemicals for soap, ink, paper, plastics, shampoo and a million other things, not to mention peanut butter. And so in 1919, the people of Coffee County, which was getting rich fast on peanuts, erected a monument. It was not a monument to George Washington Carver. But if you ride through Enterprise today you'll see on the Courthouse Square a huge boll weevil. Under it you can read the inscription:

> "In profound appreciation of the boll weevil, and of what it has done as the herald of prosperity, this monument is erected by the citizens of Enterprise, Coffee County, Alabama.

They compensated.

But compensation can't answer the deepest disappointments and the most tragic troubles. Not all failures turn into good fortune. We have to live with some of them endlessly. Trouble stalks and then stays with us. It finds a home at our home. It gets a lease on our life. Then trouble is really trouble. Then, what do you do when trouble troubles you?

The man that wanted Spain and got a prison just might have an answer for us. In that same letter to those Romans he says, *"We know that in everything God works for good with those who love him, who are called according to his purpose."* (Romans 8:28 RSV) Notice how this is **not** saying that all things that happen are good. This is saying that "in everything" (even evil things) God works for good with those who love him. So Paul says with God's help we can get:
- Beauty out of blunder,
  - Character out of conflict,
    - Fortunes out of failures
      - Opportunity out of opposition,
        - Progress out of pain,
          - Traction out of trouble, and
            - Triumph out of tragedy.

When Paul had to scratch with a pen in prison, he scratched out fourteen books of the New Testament. Paul rendered his most significant service with the leftovers of broken dreams. Few doors in life are shut without opening others. When the storm strikes a rooster, he folds up; he just endures it, wrapping his wings about him to protect himself as best he can, just drooping through to the dreary end. When the storm strikes an eagle, he has another spirit; he spreads his wings and makes the winds carry him high above the storm. The Spirit of the eagle is the Spirit of Christ.

He accepted every trouble as a divine opportunity. He transformed every ugly thing into something beautiful. Even the cross, in all its bloody Roman ugliness, meant to destroy him and his purpose forever was used by him. He didn't just endure the cross. He used it. He didn't merely bear the blows life hurled at him. He took them and turned them and made them weapons against evil. He made the destruction of the cross the salvation of the world. He took the fierce winds that beat against him and made them a force to lift people to the feet of God.

One of my former church members, Barbara Wilson Sutton, had to go to Emory Hospital for a bout with cancer. She was put in a room with a little eleven-year-old girl, Virginia Mae Daugherty, who died about a week after Barbara came home. Barbara got close enough to her while she was there to get a copy of a prayer-poem that meant more to Virginia than anything else she had. Barbara showed it to me after church and I knew I was going to need that prayer-poem for a sermon some day. I called Barbara on the phone to get a couple of sentences from it. This is what the eleven-year-old dying of cancer loved to read every day:

"My Father, I accept this sickness. I am willing to be sick as long as is necessary, whether it be for a day, a year, or until death—

Help me to believe that you are at work in every infirmity and every suffering of mine—

I believe that in all things, even this illness, you are working for good because I love you and am called to your service. Amen."
(Lionel A. Whiston)

"And God will raise you up on eagle's wings,
Bear you on the breath of dawn,
Make you to shine like the sun,
And hold you in the palm of God's hand."
(Words: Michael Joncas, 1979, Exodus 19:4, copyright 1979, 1989 North American Liturgy Resources)

PROMISE
"When We Don't Quite Make It"
Deuteronomy 3:25-28, 4:22, 34:1-12

All of these died in faith without having received the promises, but from a distance they saw and greeted them. (Hebrews 11:13)

You get up in the morning and you say, "Boy, this looks like a nice day." You're kind of happy because you're expecting your nephew and family for supper and to spend the night. You've got your list of things to get done and then your wife says, "There's something wrong with the dog."

"Well, let's get it in the car. We'll take it to the vet."

Then as you pull out to go to the vet, your wife says, "I'm feeling a little woozy, myself. Maybe it's that near stroke I had coming back on me."

"Okay, I'll take you **and** the dog."

Wife in the front, dog in her lap, headed to the Doctor first before the vet, though it was a hard choice, but then the car stalls. It must be the battery. He calls the doctor. Receptionist answers. He says, "We're going to be late. The battery's dead or something. I've got to get somebody to fix it. Would you mind calling the vet's office for me? I've got the number here, but I'll need these last two quarters to call the emergency repair service. No, maybe I just better call 911 for free and use this last fifty cents to call and cancel with my nephew."

After medics, emergency room, and drug store for prescriptions, they finally get home that night and they think about how the day started. Such a beautiful day. What happened? Life happened. You don't always make it like you intended. And if you're going to have any joy, any purpose, any peace, you're going to have to put it together out of fragments. You're not going to get twenty-four smooth hours in a row. It doesn't work that way. But the wonderful thing about it is that the Bible understands that.

Moses must have come to understand it. He didn't quite make it like he intended either. He led the children of Israel through the wilderness for a long and difficult period and finally gets them to the threshold of the Promised Land. Then Moses says to God, *"Let me go over, I pray, and see the good land beyond the Jordan."*

But God says to Moses, *"Let it suffice you, speak no more to me of this matter—You shall not go over this Jordan."* Is that us—"You're not going to get to the Promised Land? 'You shall not go over this Jordan.' In your lifetime, you're not going to get to the place of accomplishment and completion. You're not going to see in full the difference your life makes. *'You shall not go over this Jordan.'"*

When we feel this way—when life says this to us, how are we to respond? How can we escape this tragic sense of life's incompleteness? Moses hints at a part of the answer. When he learns that he won't personally get to the Promised Land, he says this to Joshua and the others who will come after him— *"For I must die in this land, I must not go over the Jordan; but you shall go over and take possession of that good land."*

We don't have to achieve it all. It's a wiser and happier person that realizes that most of the things we undertake in life must of necessity be brought to completion by someone else. So temporary frustration over our failure to complete is overcome as we charge those who come after us and know that we might thereby share in the final victory.

Years ago back in my hometown for a revival with my host pastor friend, Tom Johnson, we walked through the new educational building. As we came back from this new building we had to walk through the older, run-down educational space at the back of the old church. Tom said, "I tried to get the remodeling of this included in the whole plan, but I failed; and I'm in my last year here now. I probably won't get to see it done." But then his face brightened and he laughed a little as he said, "But I guess that's all right. I've got to leave a **little** something for the next preacher to do."

On a much deeper level, think of the young and popular President John F. Kennedy. For three years he worked hard to get proposals through congress that were his dreams for all American citizens. When he was killed by an assassin's bullet on November 22, 1963, he had failed to get through most of his major proposed legislation. Talk about a tragic sense of life's incompleteness! But what happened? The torch was passed, not just to another administration, but to the whole American People; and, in the next two years, we saw more positive legislation passed for the advancement of voting rights and human rights and basic opportunities for all than had been passed in any one Congress since the days of Washington and Lincoln.

Of course it's wrong to smother our children and attempt to make them only extensions of our own personality and pride. They have their own lives to lead. But across my ministry I've noted the joy that people take in the achievements of their children and their grandchildren. Maybe they had limited opportunities themselves, but their zest in life has come from seeing that their children had every chance.

I remember the glow on old Brother Edgar Martin's face when he came to make his little retirement speech at Annual Conference. He had served nothing but small, low-paying country circuits his entire ministry. But he spoke of seeing that his three children all had a college education. I was reminded of the look on his face when I ran into old Brother I. L. Bishop who was retired and living down at Epworth. Never stayed more than a year or two in any appointment, so discontent with the difference between his dreams for his people and their lack of vision that he always made them mad and got run off early. But he started talking about his son, Gerald, who at that time was the CEO over all our Homes for the Aged in the South Georgia Conference. His joy was something to behold.

Whether we're at work in
➢ athletics,

> ➤ or a church,
>> ➤ or a nation,
>>> ➤ or a school,
>>>> ➤ or a home,
>>>>> ➤ or a business,
>>>>>> ➤ or a simple job,

Or even if we're just trying to make it as we struggle with our health in our retirement years, it can give meaning and purpose to our labor and love if we can charge those who come after us with the completion of our tasks. *"**You** shall go over and take possession of that good land."*

The author of Hebrews, though, sums up what Moses has been pointing to as the ultimate answer for those who are troubled by the sense of life's incompleteness. When we don't quite make it, we could ponder these words. He says, (Hebrews 11:13 KJV), *"These all died in faith, not having received the promises, but having seen them afar off."* Do you sense the incompleteness of life? You can live and die in the faith that gives meaning and purpose to even an incomplete life.

It's this longing toward a goal on "The Shore Dimly Seen" that gives meaning and purpose to the present and makes ordinary men and women into giants of faith. Hebrews lists all of the great patriarchs, the early men and women who didn't completely foresee the coming of the Christian Faith that could fulfill all their strivings. And the chief point he makes is this— The giants of history and experience have been those persons that didn't have to have the assurance of complete success and achievement in their own time. They lived out their lives and worked faithfully, pointing toward a goal always just a little beyond their reach. Here's the meaning in Browning's phrase—"A man's reach should exceed his grasp, or what's a heaven for?"

Martin Luther King, Jr. referred to this Moses story in his last sermon—"I've been to the mountain. I've seen the Promised Land. Even if I don't get there with you. I've been to the mountaintop." He died before he got there. He could see it on the shore dimly seen, but he never got to the Promised Land of racial justice himself.

What made Victor Hugo, who wrote "Les Miserables," a great author? Victor Hugo said to a friend at age 70, "For half a century I have been outpouring my volumes of thought in prose, in history, philosophy, drama, romance, ode, and ballad. Yet I appear to myself not to have said a thousandth part of what is within me; and when I am laid in the tomb I shall not reckon that my life is finished."

I think he was right. Because when Day could still travel a little bit we went to New York to see "Les Miserables" on stage. Got there and our tickets were way up in a balcony that Day couldn't get to on her crutches. Kind ticket lady told us to wait a few minutes to see if some other seats became available. Sure enough, they did; and we were ushered down to about the third row where we looked right up on the stage. We got so deeply involved in that story that when Jean Valjean sang about his potential son-in-law, "Take me home! Let him live!" Day and I both dissolved into tears. And you know, every time I play a CD of Jean Valjean singing, "Take Me Home" and watch my wife quietly crying in her big automated chair on my back porch, I know Victor Hugo's still hanging around my house. People of faith never receive what was promised, but they keep working toward the promises seen afar off.

I play tennis on Friday mornings with the wife of the Psychiatrist for our Methodist Children's Home. After she gets through beating up on me, she goes to most of the schools in the blighted areas of Bibb County organizing volunteers for after school tutorial programs for kids. She has no illusions. It's tough out there. She sees all that she does as just a drop in the bucket. How do you change children's attitudes when they've been abandoned by their father, when they raise themselves while their mother works at two low-paying jobs? But she cheerfully works at the job of squeezing out that drop in the bucket because she has dreams of a full bucket one day. These kids give off hints that it's helping.

In one such school, according to Sam Shepherd, Jr., Assistant Superintendent of Schools in St. Louis, on one composition assignment for the children, the subject was, "Why You Should Be Better Than You Are." Here's what one Fourth-grader wrote:

WHY YOU SHOULD
BE BETTER THAN YOU ARE

I want to be better than I'm are because it don't mak since to be ignant and dum because I want a good education. I want to go all the way through school. I want a good decent job. That's why I'm going to be better than I'm are.

One thing is perfectly clear, and that is that the English "are" terrible. But see how this youngster is reaching out for a goal beyond the self. And because he or she is, at least one drop in the bucket may be on the way out of the slums and into a stream of life that flows toward that "deep river whose home is over Jordan."

The most perfect things in life are often but fragments—The Venus de Milo, the thirty-three years of our Master's life—The question is "How majestic is the goal?"

On the first Sunday that he was back in the pulpit of First United Methodist Church, Albany, after his wife died of a slow cancer, Dr. Leonard Cochran preached on the subject, "Georgia's Unfinished Picture." It seems that his wife, Georgia, had developed a talent for painting pictures with fish scales in a beautiful mosaic process. In her long illness with the confinement to her home, she had undertaken one especially large picture. Death overtook her before she finished it, and so there it was—Georgia's Unfinished Picture. Leonard said, "That was not her only unfinished picture. There was also her life, taken in the prime. But it's going to be finished. It's in the hands now of the Master Painter who fulfills all the promises seen afar off."

Have you ever felt that you haven't quite made it? Has life ever said to you, "You shall not go over this Jordan?" Well, some of us can charge those who come after us with the completion of our tasks. And all of us can long toward the goal on the shore dimly seen and live and die in the faith that gives meaning and purpose to even an incomplete life. Our faith sings about promises that we have seen afar off.

> O don't you want to go
> To that gospel feast,
> That Promised Land
> Where all is Peace?
> O deep river!

You may have sometimes sung, "On Jordan's stormy banks I stand and cast a wishful eye." I think that Moses and all the giants of the Faith stand on the stormy banks of the Jordan of our day and they still call out the invitation, "Oh, who will come and go with me? I am bound for the Promised Land." Will you come and go?

HOLY GROUND
"On Doing What You Have to Do"
Exodus 3:1-6, 9-10, Jeremiah 18:1-4 (NRSV)
By W. Hamp Watson, Jr.

"The vessel he was making of clay was spoiled in the potter's hand, and he reworked it into another vessel, as seemed good to him."

As he lifted his eyes, he felt his smallness. He felt like a tiny bug following a winding trail of ants because the bulk of the mountain stood there against the sky towering 8000 feet into the clouds. The sheep in front of him picked their perilous way among the rocks and he followed their zigzag path as they headed toward the West Side of the wilderness in search of tenderer young blades of grass. Suddenly a flush of hot air hit his cheeks and he fell back throwing up his arms to shield himself. His nostrils were filled with the sharp smell of smoke; his eyes almost blinded as a bright, livid flame licked and lashed out of the side of the mountain like a serpent's tongue. Then he saw the tree, the mysterious tree, like something out of Snow White and the Seven Dwarfs. It burned and gushed flame and yet no ash was forming. As time passed the tree was not burned out. It seemed only to flame up more fiercely. He was a strong man with power in every line of his body and a kind of harsh, hard courage in his face, but starting at the roots of his long hair the goose pimples formed, and the prickly fear put a chill on him in spite of the heat. Then he heard it, *"Remove your sandals from your feet, for the place on which you are standing is holy ground."*

God spoke to him then and said, *"Go Down, Moses... way down in Egypt land... tell old Pharoah... Let my people go! Behold, the cry of the people of Israel has come to me, and I have seen the oppression with which the Egyptians oppress them. Come, I will send you to Pharoah that you may bring forth my people...out of Egypt."*

So what is this "holy ground"? Is it just where bushes are burned and not consumed? I don't know how many people today would be impressed with that. Some might see it and get out their scientific minds and say, "Ah, here is a petrified tree like those in the North American desert that have been turned to stone by the centuries. And the fire—that's easily explained. This is a volcanic mountain. See that cleft in the rock by the tree. The fire and smoke in the bowels of the mountain have found a hole to escape with their fury. A tree on fire, but not burned up, so what! I see greater mysteries on the television and the Internet every day. Record it in the archeological journal if you want to, but let's pass on to more interesting things."

We have to get more of the story before we understand why it was Holy Ground. God said, "Go down, Moses!" But Moses didn't want to go. Moses was at no standard church service or youth retreat after a stirring sermon when he decided with the help of God and the preacher to go into a particular church related vocation. As a shepherd on the hillside, awed by a freak of God's nature and through the pressures of the past and his conscience and the plight of his people he is practically forced into a calling that he does not freely choose. And Moses has his suspicions about its being a call from God. He answers God, (4:1) *"But suppose they do not believe me or listen to me, but say 'The Lord did not appear to you.'"*

M oses tried every trick that we today try to get out of the responsibility that life had clearly thrust on him. He said to God, *"Who am I that I should go to Pharoah, and bring the Israelites out of Egypt?"* He tried the "too dumb" excuse, *"O my Lord, I have never been eloquent... but I am slow of speech and slow of tongue."* God seems to be pretty tolerant up to this point, but then Moses says, *"O my Lord, please send someone else."* *Then the anger of the Lord was kindled against Moses..."*

You and I have the luxury of knowing how the story came out with Moses. We know he finally accepted when he heard God say, *"Take in your hand this staff, with which you shall perform the signs."* We know *Moses took his wife and his sons, put them on a donkey and went back to the land of Egypt; and Moses carried the staff of God in his hand.* We know the holy ground for Moses was where he accepted the power of God to carry out an unchosen role in life. He began to believe God when he said, *"I will be with you"* as he began to do what he didn't want to do but had to do.

You will stand or fall as a person on the way you deal with the unchosen thing that you would all too gladly change if you could. This is true because what you do with what you have to do determines what you'll do with what you want to do. Sometimes we think about our jobs or the employment at which we labored before many of us retired. We tend to think that ours couldn't have been a God-called job because we remember all too well how we came to be in the particular line of work we followed—half choosing, but half being forced because we saw nothing else toward which we could profitably turn.

The baby gets sick and has to have hospital care and its agonized cries in the night drive us to find another job just so it has more money in it. It was the pressure of family circumstances or the call of Uncle Sam or a thousand and one other things that made us wind up where we were. It's hard to see the things that we have to do in life as the things to which God has called us. We always think of a call from God as something different from what we find ourselves inextricably fixed in.

It's not just jobs, but many roles in life are assigned to us without our asking for them. In a single month a friend of ours, a happy wife with three angelic little girls, was cast in the role of a widow. Her hospital administrator husband had a massive heart attack and died before he could get from his home to the hospital. Another friend became automatically the handler and controller of the largest grain business in the territory because a shaky aluminum canoe sent his father to a watery grave. The setting was the pond in his own front yard. Our friend doesn't like big business. His taste runs to classical music.

I have come to believe that your life will be abundant, full and meaningful according to the way you carry out roles or live through situations that you would never have chosen for yourself. One couple had a mentally deficient child and refused to face it for a long time. Then one night as they sat before the fire in their little home, they said to their preacher, "Well, if that's the way things are going to be, we'll make the best of it." That child had a limited but happy life surrounded by love and as those parents became advocates for limited children who would later become "special adults with disabilities" the spirit that birthed Agape Village and Wesley Glen in our Conference was born.

Before I married her and after she had polio, Day used to collect little teacups. We have them in a little glass-covered case between our living and dining rooms. Recently Day broke her hip and was in the Rehab where they didn't allow visiting until 4:00 P.M. I had suffered a severed Achilles tendon, and feeling a little lonely at the house I shuffled by that glass case on my crutches and just stopped to look at one particular cup. I said to the cup, "My, you're beautiful! Suddenly, the teacup spoke,

"You don't understand. I have not always been a teacup. There was a time when I was just a lump of red clay. My master took me and rolled me, pounded and patted me over and over, and I yelled out, 'Don't do that. I don't like it! Let me alone,' but he only smiled, and gently said, 'Not yet!'

Then WHAM! I was placed on a spinning wheel and suddenly I was spun around and around and around. 'Stop it! I'm getting so dizzy! I'm going to be sick!' I screamed. But the master only nodded and said, quietly, 'Not yet.' He spun me and poked and prodded and bent me out of shape to suit himself.

Then he put me in the oven. I never felt such heat. I yelled and knocked and pounded at the door. 'Help! Get me out of here!' I could see him through the opening and I could read his lips, as he shook his head from side to side, 'Not yet.'

When I thought I couldn't bear it another minute, the door opened. He carefully took me out and put me on the shelf, and I began to cool. Oh, that felt so good! 'Ah, this is much better,' I thought.

But, after I cooled, he picked me up and he brushed and painted me all over. The fumes were horrible. I thought I would gag. 'Oh, please; Stop it, Stop it!' He only shook his head and said. 'Not yet!'

Then suddenly he put me back into the oven. Only it was not like the first one. This was twice as hot and I just knew I would suffocate. I begged. I pleaded. I screamed. I cried. I was convinced I would never make it. I was ready to give up. Just then the door opened and he took me out and again placed me on the shelf, where I cooled and waited and waited, wondering what's he going to do to me next?

An hour later he handed me a mirror and said, 'Look at yourself.' And I did.

I said, 'That's not me; That couldn't be me. It's beautiful. I'm beautiful!'

He said, 'I know it hurt to be rolled and pounded and patted, but had I just left you alone, you'd have dried up. I know it made you dizzy to spin around on the wheel, but if I had stopped, you would have crumbled. I know it hurt and it was hot and disagreeable in the oven, but if I hadn't put you there, you would have cracked. I know the fumes were bad when I brushed and painted you all over, but if I hadn't done that, you never would have hardened. You wouldn't have had any color in your life.

If I hadn't put you back in that second oven, you wouldn't have survived for long because the hardness would not have held. Now you are a finished product. Now you are what I had in mind when I first began with you.'" (Circulating on the Internet from an anonymous author)

Do you understand what that means? Could that be what the hymn writer had in mind? "Thou art the potter, I am the clay."

Have you discovered your "Holy Ground" as you do what you have to do? Have you come to agree with Winston Churchill during the worst days of World War II? Somebody asked him if he thought Great Britain would have to give up. I love what he said. He said, "If you are going through Hell, don't stop."

In the name of the Father, and of the Son, and of the Holy Spirit. Amen.

PERSEVERANCE
"In Times Like These"
Psalms 11:3, Proverbs 10:25, Jeremiah 29:4-6,
II Pet 3:11,13, I Pet 1:5-7
A reflection on 9/11 by W. Hamp Watson, Jr.

"When the tempest passes, the wicked is no more, but the righteous is established forever."

Shortly after Day and I had reeled from the shock and horror of 9/11, I emailed my lawyer son in Atlanta and he responded at first by saying, "I agree that the events of today are tragic and disturbing. I am more worried, however, about the public reaction... If we do not give in to fear and if we maintain the freedom of our society, the purpose of the attack will be thwarted. Our collective reaction is more dangerous to our democracy than the attack itself, whose effect—while devastating to the victims—is limited and fleeting."

But then a little later he wrote me again and said, "By the way, my sentiments about the terrorists have darkened considerably as I have learned the extent of plot, the probable source of it, and the horrors that it caused. I now expect that we will enter an extended period of military action that will exceed the scope of Desert Storm. I expect casualties to be much higher because the rules of engagement will be much more liberal... The parties responsible for the September 11 attack may have made the same mistake as the Japanese military made at Pearl Harbor sixty years ago. They have awakened a sleeping giant and filled him with a terrible resolve. Yet the Japanese only attacked a military target for military objectives. Here, the victims were mostly civilians."

J ust how are we Christians supposed to respond? Oh, I know we'll do our part and be supportive of any effort our nation makes to bind up the nations wounds, mete out justice to the perpetrators and bring us to a time of peace and stability again. But how are we supposed to behave in times like these? The towers were toppled, the Pentagon was penetrated, and thousands of loved ones were lost in an Attack on America. It's as though the foundations have been destroyed. How are we supposed to live? The Psalmist wrestles with that question. In 11:3 he asks:

If the foundations are destroyed,
What can the righteous do?

One answer to that question is in the Psalm itself. The Psalm ends with the verse:

For the Lord is righteous;
He loves righteous deeds.

If the foundations are destroyed, what can the righteous do? Why they can just go on being righteous. Just keep on keeping on. Don't let the shock of events keep you from continuing to express your basic righteous and loving character. This inscription was found on the cornerstone of an old English Church:

"In the year 1653, when all sacred things throughout the nation were either demolished or profaned, Sir Robert Shirley Baronet founded this church, whose singular praise it is to have done the best things in the worst times and hoped them in the most calamitous."

Here was a man who in the aftermath of a bitter war and its destruction didn't despair of the good but devoted his resources to the establishment of a church. In a time of calamity and confusion he placed his hopes on the certainty and security of the causes of God. He was doing the best things in the worst times.

All across holy history God has had to raise up prophets to remind us of this basic strategy in a time of calamity. Jeremiah had to talk to the Jews who had had their whole city destroyed, most of them killed, and now they were exiles in captivity in Babylon. What marvelous, earthshaking counsel is he going to come up with? This is what he says:

Thus says the Lord of hosts, the God of Israel, to all the exiles...from Jerusalem to Babylon: Build houses and live in them; plant gardens and eat what they produce. Take wives and have sons and daughters; take wives for your sons and give your daughters in marriage, that they may bear sons and daughters; multiply there, and do not decrease. Jeremiah 29:4-6

What's this? Just keep on keeping on. Stay the course. Don't let this shocking invasion and destruction and even exile keep you from continuing your life, as you know it, producing and reproducing, growing, loving and caring. Just keep on being righteous, doing the best things in the worst times.

And here comes Peter at the end of New Testament times. He was part of a little group of courageous Christians who had the primitive expectation that God was going to dissolve the entire earth as they knew it right away, and Christ would return in the full power of the Kingdom of God while they were living. He asks this same question, but he has already given the answer even before he asks it. He says:

> *Since all these things are to be dissolved in this way, what sort of persons ought you to be in leading lives of holiness and godliness?* II Pet. 3:11.

He's already spelled out what he means by this in II Pet. 1:5-7:

> *For this very reason, you must make every effort to support your faith with goodness and goodness with knowledge, and knowledge with self-control, and self-control with endurance, and endurance with godliness, and godliness with mutual affection, and mutual affection with love.*

Think about that. At the heart of the passage— knowledge and self-control, ending with love. The cartoon of yesterday morning's "Macon Telegraph" becomes impossible for us. Did you see it? Here's a hulking blabbermouth with USA on his T-shirt saying, "Let's get even. Let's find some Arab Americans! Let's torment 'em! Let's harass 'em! Let's turn against our fellow citizens! Let's view each other with fear and suspicion, Lets--- Enter a little rat into the picture with "Terrorist" on his shirt, and he whispers into the big guy's ear, "Do precisely what I wanted you to do." Big Guy says, "Right! Do Precisely what you wanted us to ..."

No. *"When the foundations are destroyed, what then shall the righteous do?"* Why we'll just go on being righteous and caring and loving. We'll refuse to have our way of life dictated to us by terrorists. We'll do the best things in the worst times. This is the Church's business. Harry Emerson Fosdick said, "God has asked the church to tiptoe across the thin crust of hell and bring the people through." During the great holocaust of the civil war in this country Abraham Lincoln recognized this as the real spirit of the church in its best moments. In a famous speech and prayer he said, "Blessed be God who in this our great trial giveth us the churches."

You've been asked to give an offering this morning to the United Methodist Committee on Relief so that our church can respond with a network of relief workers at the scene of the tragedies in New York and Washington. Let me tell you about such a relief worker of another era who was associated with UMCOR. Bill Rose worked on an emergency relief health team near Dak To during the Viet Nam war. They would work out in the fields and hamlets during the day when they could be easily recognized as agents of mercy, but would try to get in before 5:00 P.M. when warfare started up and they might get caught in a crossfire. But Bill in his eagerness to help wounded would keep stretching the time to 6:30, sometimes 7:00.

One night about 7:00 P.M. one mile from Dak To, the Viet Cong opened fire and drove dozens of bullet holes through his land rover. With three flat tires and riding on the rims he miraculously made it back to town. Even there the Viet Cong shot up the house he was staying in and one bullet lodged in the bedstead four inches from his head. He put up a little sign, "Close Doesn't Count!" As the war ended, Bill was still in Kantoon province working in a hospital trying to patch up holes in humanity. You see, he was doing the best things in the worst times.

"When the foundations are destroyed, what shall the righteous do?" Just go on being righteous? That seems so mundane, so anticlimactic when the twin towers fall and burn and a gaping hole where loved ones once lived is left in the skyline. But who are the real heroes of our civilization? That other cartoon earlier in the week struck me. Two little boys with what look like their baseball cards for saving and trading. One says to the other, "I'll swap you two Barry Bonds and two Mark McGuires for one New York Fireman and one

New York Policeman." People just doing their jobs, just continuing to do the best things in the worst times. They could have swapped for nurses, for doctors, for counselors, for construction workers and clean-up crews. They could have swapped for many of you out there who form the fabric of this nation and civilization as you continue just to do what you can, as you keep on keeping on, doing the best things in the worst times.

Proverbs 10:25 says, *"When the tempest passes, the wicked is no more, but the righteous is established forever."* Fire burns up chaff, but it refines gold. After this newest national nightmare is ended, I wouldn't be surprised to discover that we are stronger than ever as a nation and a people. We're just a little old church with mostly older people, and it may seem that there's so little we can do. But you know as I know that the harder the times, the more the message and the ministry of the church are needed. And I somehow believe that if the church has done its job at all, times of trial and tempest will only serve to confirm us in doing the good and righteous things.

The Rev. Emmett Williams lived way into his eighties so that he lost his beloved wife, Martha Irene, before he died. Right after this he gave one of the most stirring messages I've heard in many a year at First Church Statesboro's Former Pastor Revival. Before his wife died, she and Brother Emmett were driving across the causeway down at St. Simon's Island, and a heavy fog came in. He said, "The fog is coming in mighty heavy, isn't it, Honey?"

She said, "You and I have driven through the fog many times before. Drive on, Emmett." "And you know," Brother Emmett said, "even now while I'm up here preaching to you, I seem to hear her say, "Drive on, Emmett".

By now we've all seen that smoldering site a hundred times where the rain mixed with the smoke and the stench of decomposing body parts has created a fog that hangs over our whole nation. But the Christian will just drive on through, for you see, *"When the tempest passes, the wicked is no more, but the righteous is established forever."*